taste of home
simple &
delicious
COOKBOOK

taste of home
BOOKS

REIMAN MEDIA GROUP, INC. • GREENDALE, WISCONSIN

taste of home Reader's Digest

A TASTE OF HOME/READER'S DIGEST BOOK

© 2010 Reiman Media Group, Inc.
5400 S. 60th St., Greendale WI 53129
All rights reserved.

Taste of Home and Reader's Digest are registered
trademarks of The Reader's Digest Association, Inc.

Editor in Chief: Catherine Cassidy
Vice President, Executive Editor/Books:
Heidi Reuter Lloyd
Creative Director: Ardyth Cope
U.S. Chief Marketing Officer: Lisa Karpinski
Food Director: Diane Werner RD
Senior Editor/Books: Mark Hagen
Project Editor: Julie Schnittka
Art Director: Edwin Robles, Jr.
Content Production Supervisor: Julie Wagner
Design Layout Artist: Emma Acevedo
Proofreader: Linne Bruskewitz
Recipe Asset System Manager:
Coleen Martin
Premedia Supervisor: Scott Berger
Recipe Testing & Editing:
Taste of Home Test Kitchen
Food Photography: Taste of Home Photo Studio
Administrative Assistant: Barb Czysz

The Reader's Digest Associaton, Inc.
President and Chief Executive Officer:
Mary G. Berner
President, U.S. Affinities:
Suzanne M. Grimes
SVP, Global Chief Marketing Officer:
Amy J. Radin

For other Taste of Home books and products,
visit **shoptasteofhome.com.**

For more Reader's Digest products and information,
visit **rd.com** (in the United States)
or see **rd.ca** (in Canada).

International Standard Book Number (10): 0-89821-767-9
International Standard Book Number (13): 978-0-89821-767-4
Library of Congress Control Number: 2009934707

Cover Photography
Photographers: Nancy Yuenkel, Mark Derse
Food Stylists: Jennifer Janz, Kaitlyn Besasie
Set Stylist: Jennifer Bradley Vent

Pictured on the front cover (clockwise from top center):
Pepperoni Lasagna Roll-Ups (p. 16), Chocolate Silk Pie
(p. 223), Sweet 'n' Spicy Pork Chops (p. 59) and Fiery
Spinach Chicken Salad (p. 156).

Pictured on the back cover (clockwise from top left):
Grilled Basil Chicken and Tomatoes (p. 68), Green
Beans with Red Pepper (p. 174) and Black Forest Sun-
daes (p. 195).

Additional Photo Credits:
James Peragine/Shutterstock.com (p. 4)

Printed in China
1 3 5 7 9 10 8 6 4 2

table of contents

introduction

This book's mouthwatering menus and useful shopping lists make grocery shopping and weekday cooking simple and delicious.

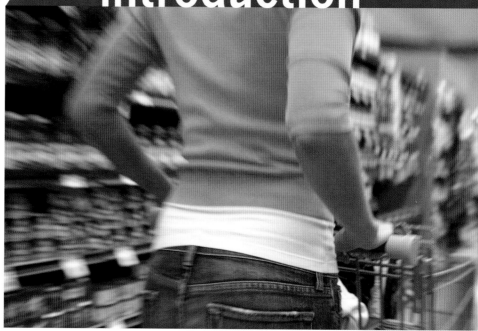

Tasty family dinners take no time at all...

Coming up with dinner ideas day after day can be a challenge. The dishes not only need to be quick and easy for the cook, they also have to be flavorful and satisfying for the family. Where can frustrated folks turn? To this **Simple & Delicious Cookbook!**

Easy meal planning begins with the entree. Our Test Kitchen recipe specialists have done the time-consuming task of designing dinners for you by putting together 12 weeks of sure-to-please main dishes. Harried home cooks can rely on those 60 family-favorite recipes for almost 3 months! And to save you even more time, we've put together weekly shopping lists of the ingredients you'll need to make the enticing entrees. (Look for the Weekday Meals starting on page 7.)

This one-of-a-kind cookbook also features Breakfast, Soups & Sandwiches, Salads & Sides and Desserts chapters to help you round out the Weekday Meals. Mix and match these dishes any way you want to create an endless assortment of timeless and tasty meals.

With **Simple & Delicious**, fantastic, fuss-free meals—week after week—are right at your fingertips!

Mix and Match

The Weekday Meals chapter supplies you with 60 main dishes. Now what to serve with them? The rest of the **Simple & Delicious Cookbook** offers 182 appealing accompaniments to pair with the enticing entrees. Flip to soups, salads and sides for a perfect partner. Then, breeze through the desserts for a sweet ending to your family meal. With so many pleasing possibilities, you'll never again be stuck with a "What's for Dinner?" dilemma.

Hundreds of helpful hints

Recipes throughout the book feature this timely tip icon, which offers ideas for reducing preparation time, tricks for buying and storing ingredients and secrets for substituting ingredients.

Timely recipes

Many of this cookbook's recipes take a mere **30** minutes to prepare. And some can be ready in just **20** or **10** minutes! These fast-to-fix dishes are indicated with icons, like those pictured at right. No matter how much (or how little) time you have on your hands, you'll find the preparation and cooking times displayed for every recipe in the book.

Storing Pantry Staples

Keeping your pantry well-stocked will speed up meal preparation. Unopened items should be used by their use-by dates. For opened items, follow the guidelines below. In the pantry, store opened items tightly closed and place in a cool, dry place (around 70°). Refrigerator temperatures should be between 34°-40°. For best quality, foods should be frozen at 0°.

Opened Food Item	Pantry	Refrigerator	Freezer
Baking powder	18 months		
Baking soda	18 months		
Bouillon cubes	1 year		
Bread	2 to 7 days	4 to 7 days	3 months
Canned goods			
Fish and Seafood		2 days	
Fruit	1 week		
Pasta Sauces		5 days	
Vegetables		2 to 3 days	
Chili sauce		4 to 6 months	
Cornmeal	1 year		
Cornstarch	18 months		
Dried fruit	6 months		
Flour			
All-purpose	15 months		
Whole Wheat	6 months		
Honey	1 year		
Jam and jelly		1 year	
Ketchup		4 to 6 months	
Mayonnaise		2 months	
Mustard		6 to 12 months	
Nuts	3 to 6 months	3 to 6 months	6 to 12 months
Oils			
Canola or corn oil	6 months		
Olive oil	4 months		
Peanut butter	2 to 3 months		
Pickles		1 to 2 months	
Rice			
Brown	1 month	6 months	
White	2 years		
Salad dressings		3 months	
Salsa		1 month	
Shortening	8 months		
Soy sauce		1 year	
Sugar			
Brown	4 months		
Granulated	2 years		
Worcestershire sauce	1 year		

thursday's dish

MONDAY   TUESDAY   WEDNESDAY   FRIDAY

GROCERIES/

- ☐ 1-1/2 pounds boneless beef top round *or* beef sirloin steak
- ☐ 1-1/2 pounds boneless skinless chicken breasts
- ☐ 6 boneless pork loin chops (1/2 inch thick and 6 ounces *each*)
- ☐ 4 salmon fillets (6 ounces *each*)
- ☐ 2 cups cubed cooked turkey
- ☐ 1 cup cubed fully cooked ham
- ☐ 1 pound broccoli
- ☐ 2 large onions
- ☐ 1 cup cherry tomatoes
- ☐ Fresh cilantro
- ☐ 1 sweet red pepper
- ☐ 1 green pepper
- ☐ 6 green onions
- ☐ 1 jalapeno pepper
- ☐ 1/2 pound sliced fresh mushrooms
- ☐ 2 cups chopped seedless watermelon
- ☐ 1-1/2 cups cubed fresh pineapple
- ☐ 1 can (15 ounces) apricot halves
- ☐ 1 can (14-1/2 ounces) Mexican diced tomatoes
- ☐ 1 can (11 ounces) mandarin oranges
- ☐ Dried cranberries
- ☐ Orange juice
- ☐ 1 can (10-3/4 ounces) condensed cream of mushroom soup
- ☐ Sherry
- ☐ 1/4 cup shredded Swiss cheese
- ☐ 1/4 cup shredded Mexican cheese blend
- ☐ Tortilla chips

STAPLES/

- Beef broth *or* beef bouillon
- Butter
- Canola oil
- Chicken broth *or* chicken bouillon
- Chili powder
- Cornstarch
- Garlic cloves
- Ground allspice
- Ground cumin
- Lime juice
- Paprika
- Pasta (linguine)
- Pepper
- Rice
- Salt
- Soy sauce

30-minute shopping spree!

Have a plan of action when heading out to the grocery store each week. First, stock up on canned goods and boxed foods. Then head to the produce, meat and refrigerated areas for perishable goods. Make the frozen foods section your last stop, especially during warm weather. In less than 30 minutes, you should be able to net all the basics for a full week of meals.

Apricot slices give a burst of fruit flavor to this sensational stir-fry.

SUSAN PAYNE
CORNER BROOK
NEWFOUNDLAND

Freeze Leftover Rice:
When preparing rice, make extra. Packaged in heavy-duty resealable plastic bags, cooked rice will keep in the freezer for up to 6 months. To reheat, add 2 tablespoons of liquid for each cup of rice; microwave or cook in a saucepan until heated through.

 apricot beef stir-fry

PREP/TOTAL TIME: 20 MIN.

1	can (15 ounces) apricot halves
2	tablespoons cornstarch
3/4	cup beef broth
2	tablespoons soy sauce
1-1/2	pounds boneless beef top round *or* beef sirloin steak, cut into thin strips
1	tablespoon canola oil
2	cups fresh broccoli florets
1/2	cup chopped onion
1	cup cherry tomatoes

Hot cooked rice

Drain apricots, reserving 1/4 cup juice. Cut apricots in quarters and set aside. In a small bowl, whisk the cornstarch, broth, soy sauce and reserved juice until smooth; set aside.

In a large skillet or wok, stir-fry beef in oil for 3 minutes. Add broccoli and onion; stir-fry 2-3 minutes longer or until vegetables are crisp-tender. Stir sauce and add to the pan. Bring to a boil; cook and stir for 2 minutes or until thickened. Add tomatoes and reserved apricots; cook until heated through. Serve over rice. **Yield:** 6 servings.

Bring a bit of the Southwest to your table with this spirit-warming soup. Loaded with tender chicken, diced tomatoes and plenty of seasonings, it's sure to be requested again and again.

TASTE OF HOME TEST KITCHEN

Skip the Cilantro: With its slightly sharp flavor, cilantro gives dishes a distinct taste. If you and your family don't care for it, simply use parsley instead.

chicken tortilla soup 20〉

PREP/TOTAL TIME: 20 MIN.

1	cup chopped onion
1	teaspoon minced garlic
3	cups chicken broth
1	can (14-1/2 ounces) Mexican diced tomatoes
1/2	teaspoon chili powder
1/4	teaspoon ground cumin
1-1/2	pounds boneless skinless chicken breasts, cubed
2	tablespoons cornstarch
1/4	cup cold water
1/4	cup shredded Mexican cheese blend
1	tablespoon minced fresh cilantro

Tortilla chips, optional

In a large saucepan, combine the first six ingredients; bring to a boil. Add chicken. Reduce heat; cover and simmer for 4-6 minutes or until chicken is no longer pink. Combine cornstarch and water until smooth; gradually stir into soup.

Bring to a boil; cook and stir for 1 minute or until thickened. Top servings with cheese and cilantro. Serve with tortilla chips if desired. **Yield:** 6 servings.

My family loves the taste of these moist and spicy pork chops.

MARGARET WILSON
HEMET
CALIFORNIA

Easy Pasta Side Dish:  Orzo pasta is a quick side for weekday dinners. Cook orzo according to package directions. Meanwhile, in a large skillet, saute 1 minced garlic clove in 2 tablespoons oil and 2 tablespoons butter. Drain orzo; add to the skillet. Season with salt and pepper.

③⓪⟩ cranberry-orange pork chops

PREP/TOTAL TIME: 25 MIN.

6	boneless pork loin chops (1/2 inch thick and 6 ounces *each*)
1/4	teaspoon salt
1/4	teaspoon pepper
1	tablespoon canola oil
1/2	cup chicken broth
1	can (11 ounces) mandarin oranges, drained
1/3	cup dried cranberries
1/4	teaspoon ground allspice
1/4	teaspoon paprika

Sprinkle the pork chops with salt and pepper. In a large skillet, brown the chops in oil on both sides.

Add the remaining ingredients. Bring to a boil. Reduce heat; cover and simmer for 8-10 minutes or until a meat thermometer reads 160°. **Yield:** 6 servings.

A fresh fruit salsa complements the meaty texture of salmon. It's easy enough for weekdays, yet special enough for company.

TASTE OF HOME TEST KITCHEN

Select Your Salmon: Salmon is readily available cut into skinless and boneless fillets or into steaks. You can use either in this recipe.

salmon with fruit salsa

PREP: 15 MIN. + STANDING GRILL: 15 MIN.

2	cups chopped seedless watermelon
1-1/2	cups cubed fresh pineapple
1/3	cup chopped sweet red pepper
1/4	cup chopped green onions
1/4	cup minced fresh cilantro
1/4	cup orange juice
1/4	cup lime juice
1	teaspoon chopped jalapeno pepper
1/2	teaspoon salt, *divided*
1/4	teaspoon pepper, *divided*
4	salmon fillets (6 ounces *each*)

In a large bowl, combine the first eight ingredients; add 1/4 teaspoon salt and 1/8 teaspoon pepper. Let stand at room temperature for at least 30 minutes.

Coat grill rack with cooking spray before starting the grill. Sprinkle salmon with remaining salt and pepper. Place on grill rack. Grill, covered, over medium heat for 6-9 minutes on each side or until fish flakes easily with a fork. Serve the salsa with a slotted spoon with salmon. **Yield:** 4 servings.

EDITOR'S NOTE: When cutting hot peppers, disposable gloves are recommended. Avoid touching your face.

This creamy pasta is a great use for extra turkey and ham. It's a family favorite.

SANDRA NETHERTON
MARIETTA, GEORGIA

Shopping for Ham:  When you need a cup or so of cubed ham, ask the person behind your grocery store's deli counter to cut a piece about 1 in. thick. Then simply cube it at home.

30 > turkey cordon bleu pasta

PREP/TOTAL TIME: 30 MIN.

2 cups sliced fresh mushrooms
1/2 cup sliced green onions
1/4 cup chopped green pepper
2 tablespoons butter
2 cups cubed cooked turkey
1 cup cubed fully cooked ham
1 can (10-3/4 ounces) condensed cream of mushroom soup, undiluted
1/2 cup water
1/4 cup sherry *or* chicken broth
Hot cooked linguine
1/4 cup shredded Swiss cheese

In a large skillet, saute the mushrooms, onions and green pepper in butter for 4-5 minutes or until crisp-tender.

In a large bowl, combine the turkey, ham, soup, water and sherry. Stir into vegetables. Bring to a boil. Reduce heat to medium; cook, uncovered, for 3-4 minutes or until heated through. Serve with linguine. Sprinkle with cheese. **Yield:** 4 servings.

wednesday's dish

MONDAY TUESDAY THURSDAY FRIDAY

offer an assortment of main courses...

Beef...chicken...sausage...seafood...pasta...rice. By mixing up your main-dish offerings, you can keep weekday dinners interesting for your family. Surprise them with a quick-as-a-wink recipe (like Beef Burgundy Baskets) that looks like you spent hours in the kitchen! Or take it easy on yourself some especially busy day by making satisfying sandwiches.

GROCERIES/

- [ ] 2 packages (17 ounces each) refrigerated beef tips with gravy
- [ ] 2 cups cubed cooked chicken
- [ ] 24 slices pepperoni
- [ ] 1/2 pound cooked kielbasa or Polish sausage
- [ ] 3/4 pound uncooked medium shrimp
- [ ] 2 medium ripe avocados
- [ ] Fresh chives
- [ ] 1 cucumber
- [ ] 1 lemon
- [ ] Lettuce leaves
- [ ] 2 cups whole fresh mushrooms
- [ ] 1/2 pound sliced fresh mushrooms
- [ ] 8 green onions
- [ ] 1 large onion
- [ ] 1 red onion
- [ ] 2 green peppers
- [ ] 1 sweet red pepper
- [ ] 1 large tomato
- [ ] 1 package (16 ounces) penne pasta
- [ ] 1 package (16 ounces) lasagna noodles
- [ ] 1 jar (16 ounces) pearl onions
- [ ] Burgundy wine
- [ ] White wine
- [ ] 1 jar capers
- [ ] 1 jar meatless spaghetti sauce
- [ ] 1 can (14-1/2 ounces) diced tomatoes
- [ ] 1 package (10 ounces) frozen puff pastry shells
- [ ] 1/2 pint heavy whipping cream
- [ ] 1 carton (15 ounces) ricotta cheese
- [ ] 3 slices Swiss cheese
- [ ] 1 package (8 ounces) cream cheese
- [ ] Shredded Parmesan
- [ ] 6 whole grain bagels

STAPLES/

- Canola oil ▪ Bay leaf ▪ Butter ▪ Chicken broth or chicken bouillon ▪ Chili powder ▪ Dried basil ▪ Dried oregano ▪ Dried thyme ▪ Flour ▪ Garlic cloves ▪ Hot pepper sauce ▪ Italian seasoning ▪ Pepper ▪ Rice ▪ Salt

Dress up refrigerated beef tips in gravy by stirring in pearl onions and mushrooms.

TASTE OF HOME TEST KITCHEN

Skip the Slicing: Instead of buying whole mushrooms and cutting them in half, buy an 8-ounce package of sliced mushrooms and reduce the cooking time.

beef burgundy baskets

PREP/TOTAL TIME: 30 MIN.

1	package (10 ounces) frozen puff pastry shells
2	cups whole fresh mushrooms, cut in half
2	tablespoons canola oil
1	jar (16 ounces) pearl onions, drained
2	packages (17 ounces *each*) refrigerated beef tips with gravy
1/4	cup burgundy wine
1	teaspoon dried thyme

Bake pastry shells according to package directions. In a large skillet, cook mushrooms in oil for 2-3 minutes or until browned. Add onions; cook for 1 minute. Add the beef tips with gravy, wine and thyme; heat through. Carefully remove top of pastry shells; fill with beef mixture. **Yield:** 6 servings.

Rich, creamy and laced with wine, this chicken-and-pasta main dish is a family favorite. Who'd guess it's so quick and easy?

**ELAINE MOSER
SPOKANE
WASHINGTON**

Cooking Capers: Pickled in wine, vinegar or brine, capers lend a salty, lemony flavor to sauces, salads, veggies and main dishes. They can be found on grocery store shelves with olives and pickles.

creamy chicken and pasta

PREP/TOTAL TIME: 30 MIN.

2 cups uncooked penne pasta
2 cups sliced fresh mushrooms
1 cup sliced green onions
2 tablespoons butter
1/2 cup white wine *or* chicken broth
1 teaspoon minced garlic
1 tablespoon all-purpose flour
1/3 cup water
1 cup heavy whipping cream
2 cups cubed cooked chicken
2 tablespoons capers, drained
1/4 teaspoon salt
1/8 teaspoon pepper
Shredded Parmesan cheese

Cook pasta according to package directions. Meanwhile, in a large skillet, saute mushrooms and onions in butter for 4-5 minutes or until tender. Add wine or broth and garlic. Bring to a boil; cook until liquid is reduced by half, about 5 minutes.

Combine the flour and water until smooth; gradually add to the mushroom mixture. Bring to a boil. Reduce heat; cook and stir for 2 minutes or until thickened. Stir in the cream. Bring to a boil. Reduce the heat; simmer, uncovered, for 4-5 minutes or until heated through.

Drain pasta. Add the pasta, chicken, capers, salt and pepper to cream sauce. Cook for 3-4 minutes or until heated through. Sprinkle with Parmesan cheese. **Yield:** 5 servings.

After finding I had some leftover items from making lasagna, I came up with this recipe.

**JENNIFER JUDAY
COPPERAS COVE
TEXAS**

Other Use for Pepperoni: Buy a large package of sliced pepperoni. Use some here and some in Mozzarella Beef Roll-Ups on page 33.

pepperoni lasagna roll-ups

PREP: 25 MIN. BAKE: 25 MIN.

3	lasagna noodles
3/4	cup ricotta cheese
1/2	teaspoon minced chives
1/2	teaspoon dried oregano
1/2	teaspoon dried basil
24	slices pepperoni
3	slices Swiss cheese, cut into thirds
1	cup meatless spaghetti sauce
1/4	cup shredded Parmesan cheese

Cook the noodles according to package directions; drain. Combine the ricotta cheese, chives, oregano and basil; spread 1/4 cup over each noodle to within 1/2 in. of edges. Top with the pepperoni and Swiss cheese; carefully roll up.

Place seam side down in a greased shallow 1-qt. baking dish; top with spaghetti sauce. Cover and bake at 350° for 20-25 minutes or until bubbly.

Sprinkle roll-ups with the Parmesan cheese. Let stand for 5 minutes before serving. **Yield:** 3 servings.

I've made this hearty dish with all shrimp or with all turkey sausage, and it's just as good.

MRS. LEO MERCHANT
JACKSON
MISSISSIPPI

 Frozen Fish Fact: If you only have frozen shrimp on hand, thaw completely before using in this recipe. Otherwise, the other ingredients might become overcooked before the shrimp is thawed and heated through.

quick shrimp gumbo 20

PREP/TOTAL TIME: 20 MIN.

1 cup finely chopped onion
3 garlic cloves, minced
1 teaspoon canola oil
1/2 pound cooked kielbasa *or* Polish sausage, halved and cut into 1/4-inch slices
1-1/2 cups chopped green pepper
1 can (14-1/2 ounces) diced tomatoes, undrained
1 cup chicken broth
1 bay leaf
1 teaspoon Italian seasoning
1/2 teaspoon salt
1/2 teaspoon chili powder
1/4 teaspoon pepper
1/8 teaspoon hot pepper sauce
3/4 pound uncooked medium shrimp, peeled and deveined

1/2 cup uncooked instant rice
Lemon slices, optional

In a large saucepan, saute onion and garlic in oil for 2 minutes or until crisp-tender. Stir in sausage; cook and stir for 2 minutes or until sausage begins to brown. Add green pepper; cook and stir for 2 minutes or until crisp-tender. Stir in the tomatoes, broth, seasonings and hot pepper sauce. Bring to a boil.

Cook, uncovered, for 2 minutes or until heated through. Stir in shrimp. Cook 3-4 minutes longer or until shrimp turn pink. Stir in rice. Remove from the heat.

Cover and let stand for 5 minutes or until rice is tender. Discard bay leaf. Serve with lemon slices if desired. **Yield:** 4 servings.

Here's a tasty meatless sandwich I concocted by combining some of our family's favorite ingredients—garlic, avocado, cream cheese and bagels. Leftover spread makes an excellent veggie dip.

**TRICIA FARNUM
BRANSON WEST
MISSOURI**

Vary the Flavor: Stir fresh chives or minced sun-dried tomato into the cream cheese.

30 › zesty garlic-avocado sandwiches

PREP/TOTAL TIME: 30 MIN.

1	package (8 ounces) cream cheese, softened
2	medium ripe avocados, peeled
1	garlic clove, minced
1/8	teaspoon salt
6	whole grain bagels, split and toasted
6	slices tomato
1/2	cup sliced cucumber
6	slices red onion
6	sweet red pepper rings
6	lettuce leaves

In a small bowl, beat the cream cheese, avocados, garlic and salt until smooth. Spread on bagels; top with tomato, cucumber, onion, pepper rings and lettuce. **Yield:** 6 servings.

friday's dish

MONDAY TUESDAY WEDNESDAY THURSDAY

GROCERIES/

- ☐ 1-1/2 pounds shaved fully cooked ham
- ☐ 3/4 pound boneless skinless chicken breasts
- ☐ 4 salmon fillets (6 ounces each)
- ☐ 8 slices uncooked turkey breast
- ☐ 1 beef flank steak (1 pound)
- ☐ 1 each medium green, sweet red and yellow pepper
- ☐ 2 medium ears sweet corn
- ☐ 1 package (5 ounces) spring mix salad greens
- ☐ 1 large tomato
- ☐ 1 small onion
- ☐ 1 red onion
- ☐ Fresh parsley
- ☐ 3 cups meatless spaghetti sauce
- ☐ 1 jar capers
- ☐ 1 package (9 to 10 ounces) frozen chopped spinach
- ☐ 4 slices Swiss cheese
- ☐ Shredded cheddar cheese
- ☐ Shredded Parmesan
- ☐ 6 hamburger buns
- ☐ 4 flour tortillas (6 inches)

STAPLES/

■ Balsamic vinegar ■ Brown sugar ■ Chili powder ■ Chili sauce ■ Dill weed ■ Dried oregano ■ Garlic cloves ■ Garlic powder ■ Grated Parmesan cheese ■ Ground cloves ■ Ground cumin ■ Lemon juice ■ Mayonnaise ■ Mustard (Dijon and any prepared) ■ Oil (canola and olive) ■ Pepper ■ Seasoned bread crumbs ■ Salt ■ Soy sauce ■ Worcestershire sauce

tasty menus are sure to please...

Who'll be happier with this week's menu plan...you or your family? Your famished clan will certainly enjoy sitting down to any of these mouthwatering meals. But you're sure to love each dish's ease of preparation. For fitting finales to these tasty dinners, turn to the luscious dessert options beginning on page 193!

My mother would buy the ham and make a batch of sauce on Saturday. Then after church on Sunday, our hungry family would be able to have a fast meal.

MOLLIE FRY
RALEIGH
NORTH CAROLINA

30) barbecue ham sandwiches

PREP/TOTAL TIME: 25 MIN.

1	cup plus 2 tablespoons chili sauce
3/4	cup packed brown sugar
1/2	cup plus 1 tablespoon water
3/4	teaspoon prepared mustard
1/4	to 1/2 teaspoon chili powder
1/8	teaspoon ground cloves
1-1/2	pounds shaved fully cooked ham
6	hamburger buns, split and toasted

In a large saucepan, combine the first six ingredients. Cook, uncovered, over low heat for 15 minutes. Stir in ham; heat through. Using a slotted spoon, serve on buns. **Yield:** 6 servings.

SPEEDY BEAN SALAD:

For a fast side dish for sandwiches, combine a 15-ounce can of rinsed and drained chickpeas and a 15-ounce can of rinsed and drained black beans. Stir in some chopped bell peppers; drizzle with bottled balsamic vinaigrette.

Our family loves the spicy flavor of these fajitas. I also appreciate the fact that they're fast to fix.

ELEANOR MARTENS
ROSENORT
MANITOBA

Slicing Secret: To ensure even cooking, slice the onions and peppers so that they are the same size.

chicken veggie fajitas 20〉

PREP/TOTAL TIME: 20 MIN.

3	tablespoons lemon juice
1	tablespoon soy sauce
1	tablespoon Worcestershire sauce
2	teaspoons canola oil
1	garlic clove, minced
1/2	teaspoon ground cumin
1/2	teaspoon dried oregano
3/4	pound boneless skinless chicken breasts, cut into 1/2-inch strips
1	small onion, sliced and separated into rings
1/2	*each* medium green, sweet red and yellow pepper, julienned
4	flour tortillas (6 inches), warmed

Shredded cheddar cheese, optional

In a small bowl, combine the first seven ingredients. Place chicken and vegetables in a single layer in a greased 15-in. x 10-in. x 1-in. baking pan; drizzle with 1/4 cup lemon juice mixture. Broil 4-6 in. from the heat for 4 minutes.

Turn chicken and vegetables; drizzle with the remaining lemon juice mixture. Broil 4 minutes longer or until chicken juices run clear. Serve on tortillas with cheese if desired. **Yield:** 4 servings.

You won't need to fish for compliments when this eye-catching main course appears on the table. The dill and mustard topping pairs well with the salmon.

TASTE OF HOME TEST KITCHEN

pecan brussels sprouts, pg. 158

30› salmon with dijon mayonnaise

PREP/TOTAL TIME: 25 MIN.

4	salmon fillets (6 ounces *each*)
1/2	cup mayonnaise
2	tablespoons grated Parmesan cheese
1	tablespoon Dijon mustard
1/4	teaspoon dill weed

Place the salmon skin side down on a greased broiler pan. Broil 4 in. from the heat for 10-16 minutes or until fish flakes easily with a fork.

Meanwhile, combine the remaining ingredients in a small bowl. Serve with the salmon. **Yield:** 4 servings.

SKINLESS SALMON: (tip)

To remove the skin from salmon before using, bring 1/2 inch of water to a slow boil in a frying pan. Put the salmon, skin side down, in the water for a minute. Carefully remove the salmon from the water; peel off the skin. Gently rinse the fish and proceed with the recipe.

lemon angel hair, pg. 164

For this main course, I tuck Swiss cheese and spinach into browned turkey slices, then top them with store-bought spaghetti sauce before baking.

**LILLIAN BUTLER
STRATFORD
CONNECTICUT**

tip

Squeezing Spinach Dry: To prevent this dish from becoming watery, it's important to completely dry the thawed frozen spinach. Drain the spinach in a colander. With clean hands, squeeze out the water.

turkey florentine

PREP/TOTAL TIME: 30 MIN.

1 cup seasoned bread crumbs
8 slices uncooked turkey breast
2 tablespoons canola oil
4 slices Swiss cheese, cut in half
1 package (9 to 10 ounces) frozen chopped spinach, thawed and squeezed dry
3 cups meatless spaghetti sauce

Place bread crumbs in a large resealable plastic bag; add turkey in batches and shake to coat. In a large skillet, brown turkey in oil over medium heat. Remove from the skillet.

Place half a cheese slice and 2 tablespoons spinach down the center of each turkey slice. Fold turkey over filling; secure with toothpicks.

Place in a greased 11-in. x 7-in. baking dish. Top with spaghetti sauce. Bake, uncovered, at 400° for 12-15 minutes or turkey juices run clear. Discard toothpicks. **Yield:** 4 servings.

Balsamic vinaigrette makes this fresh salad explode with flavor.

TIFFANY MARTINEZ
ALISO VIEJO
CALIFORNIA

Cold Corn Kernels:  One cup frozen corn kernels can be used in place of the ears of corn. Cook and drain as directed.

30 ⟩ veggie steak salad
PREP/TOTAL TIME: 30 MIN.

2 medium ears sweet corn, husks and silk removed
1 beef flank steak (1 pound)
1/4 teaspoon salt
1/4 teaspoon pepper
1/4 cup olive oil, *divided*
2 tablespoons balsamic vinegar
1 teaspoon garlic powder
1 teaspoon capers, drained
1 teaspoon Dijon mustard
1 package (5 ounces) spring mix salad greens
1 large tomato, chopped
4 slices red onion, separated into rings
1/4 cup minced fresh parsley
1/4 cup shredded Parmesan cheese

In a Dutch oven, bring 8 cups of water to a boil. Add corn; boil 5-7 minutes or until tender. Drain and immediately place corn in ice water for about 10 minutes. Drain and pat dry; cut the kernels from the cobs.

Meanwhile, rub steak with salt and pepper. In a large skillet, cook steak in 2 tablespoons oil for 6-8 minutes on each side or until meat reaches desired doneness (for medium-rare, a meat thermometer should read 145°; medium, 160°; well-done, 170°).

For dressing, combine the vinegar, garlic powder, capers, mustard and remaining oil in a jar with a tight-fitting lid; shake well.

Thinly slice beef across the grain. In a large bowl, combine the salad greens, tomato, onion, parsley, corn and beef. Drizzle with dressing; toss to coat. Sprinkle with Parmesan cheese. **Yield:** 5 servings.

friday's dish

MONDAY TUESDAY WEDNESDAY THURSDAY

GROCERIES/

- ☐ 2 cups cubed cooked turkey breast
- ☐ 2 packages (12 ounces each) refrigerated breaded chicken breast tenders
- ☐ 1 pound boneless beef sirloin steak
- ☐ 4 halibut steaks (6 ounces each)
- ☐ 1 pork tenderloin (1 pound)
- ☐ 2 medium sweet red peppers
- ☐ 1 medium sweet yellow pepper
- ☐ Fresh mint
- ☐ Fresh gingerroot
- ☐ 1 medium onion
- ☐ 12 ounces fettuccine
- ☐ 1 jar (12 ounces) roasted sweet red peppers
- ☐ 1 can (8 ounces) tomato sauce
- ☐ 1 jar (8 ounces) giardiniera
- ☐ 1 can (14-1/2 ounces) diced tomatoes
- ☐ 1 jar (10 ounces) peach preserves
- ☐ 1 jar (10 ounces) peach spreadable fruit
- ☐ 1 can (8-1/4 ounces) sliced peaches in extra-light syrup
- ☐ 1 package (16 ounces) frozen chopped broccoli
- ☐ 1 package (8 ounces) cream cheese
- ☐ 1/2 cup garlic-herb cheese spread
- ☐ Shredded Parmesan
- ☐ 8 slices part-skim mozzarella cheese
- ☐ 8 slices Italian bread

STAPLES/

- ▪ Balsamic vinegar ▪ Butter
- ▪ Chicken broth or chicken bouillon ▪ Dijon mustard
- ▪ Garlic cloves ▪ Italian seasoning ▪ Milk ▪ Olive oil
- ▪ Pepper ▪ Salt

time-saving meal helpers...

When writing down grocery list items, be sure to include convenient products to easily round out your meals. For instance, purchase frozen chopped onions and green peppers to save time while preparing meals. Stock up on frozen vegetables, refrigerated breads and boxed rice or pasta mixes to round out your from-scratch main dishes.

This is one of my family's favorite turkey dishes. There are never any leftovers. I like it because it's quick, light and delicious.

PAULA MARCHESI
LENHARTSVILLE
PENNSYLVANIA

Rely on Roasted Red Peppers:
Roasted red peppers add color and a slight smoky flavor to a variety of dishes. Use 1/2 cup in the recipe here and the remainder in Cuban-Style Stuffed Peppers on page 39.

30 › creamy turkey fettuccine

PREP/TOTAL TIME: 30 MIN.

12	ounces uncooked fettuccine
3/4	cup milk
4	ounces cream cheese, cubed
1/2	cup garlic-herb cheese spread
2	cups cubed cooked turkey breast
3	cups frozen chopped broccoli, thawed
1/2	cup chopped roasted sweet red peppers
1/2	cup shredded Parmesan cheese, *divided*
1/4	teaspoon pepper

Cook fettuccine according to package directions. Meanwhile, in a large saucepan, combine the milk, cream cheese and cheese spread. Cook and stir over medium heat until cheeses are melted and mixture is smooth. Stir in the turkey, broccoli, roasted peppers, 1/4 cup Parmesan cheese and pepper; heat through.

Drain fettuccine and place in a large serving bowl. Top with turkey mixture; toss gently to coat. Sprinkle with remaining Parmesan cheese. **Yield:** 6 servings.

Pickled vegetables add a little zest to ordinary chicken sandwiches. You can also cook them on an indoor panini grill.

TASTE OF HOME TEST KITCHEN

Pick-Up Some Giardiniera! Giardiniera, a pickled vegetable mixture, is available in mild and hot varieties and can be found in the Italian or pickle section of your grocery store.

garden chicken panini 20

PREP/TOTAL TIME: 20 MIN.

2   packages (12 ounces *each*) refrigerated breaded chicken breast tenders
1/4 cup butter, softened
8   slices Italian bread
1/4 cup tomato sauce
1/4 cup giardiniera
8   slices part-skim mozzarella cheese

Heat chicken tenders in the microwave according to package directions. Butter one side of each slice of bread. Place four slices, buttered side down, on a griddle or panini grill. Spread each slice with 1 tablespoon tomato sauce; top with two to three chicken tenders, 1 tablespoon giardiniera and two slices of cheese. Top with remaining bread, butter side up. Cook over medium heat until golden brown, turning once if using a griddle. **Yield:** 4 servings.

Thin tender strips of sirloin steak are served with sauteed sweet peppers and onion in this pleasing entree.

**NANCY SAFFIELD
PASADENA
MARYLAND**

Easy Italian Seasoning: For each teaspoon of Italian seasoning, substitute 1/4 teaspoon each of basil, thyme, rosemary and oregano.

30 italian pepper steak

PREP/TOTAL TIME: 25 MIN.

1   teaspoon Italian seasoning, *divided*
1/2 teaspoon salt, *divided*
1/2 teaspoon pepper, *divided*
1   pound boneless beef sirloin steak, trimmed
1   medium sweet red pepper, julienned
1   medium sweet yellow pepper, julienned
1   medium onion, julienned
6   garlic cloves, peeled and thinly sliced
1   tablespoon olive oil
1   can (14-1/2 ounces) diced tomatoes, drained
1   teaspoon balsamic vinegar

In a small bowl, combine 1/2 teaspoon Italian seasoning, 1/4 teaspoon salt and 1/4 teaspoon pepper. Rub mixture over both sides of steak; set aside.

In a large nonstick skillet, saute the peppers, onion and garlic in oil until vegetables are crisp-tender. Stir in the tomatoes and remaining Italian seasoning, salt and pepper. Reduce the heat; cover and simmer for 5 minutes. Remove from the heat. Stir in the vinegar; keep warm.

Place steak on a broiler pan coated with cooking spray. Broil 4-6 in. from the heat for 4-8 minutes on each side or until the meat reaches desired doneness (for medium-rare, a meat thermometer should read 145°; medium, 160°; well-done, 170°). Let stand for 5 minutes before slicing; serve with the vegetable mixture. **Yield:** 4 servings.

I knew this golden entree was a winner when my mother-in-law—who owns every cookbook imaginable—asked for the recipe! Halibut steaks are flavored with a deliciously different sauce that combines fresh mint and peach preserves.

DAWN MAYFORD
GRANITE CITY
ILLINOIS

minty peach halibut 20⟩

PREP/TOTAL TIME: 20 MIN.

1	jar (10 ounces) peach preserves
2	teaspoons minced fresh mint
4	halibut steaks (6 ounces *each*)
1/2	teaspoon salt
1/4	teaspoon pepper

In a small saucepan, combine the preserves and mint. Bring to a boil; cook and stir for 2 minutes. Remove from the heat; set aside. Sprinkle fish with salt and pepper.

Broil 4 in. from the heat for 5 minutes. Spoon half of peach mixture over fish. Broil 1 minute longer; turn. Broil 3-4 minutes more or until fish flakes easily with a fork, basting once with remaining peach mixture. **Yield:** 4 servings.

COOKING FISH:

Overcooked fish loses its flavor and becomes tough. As a general guideline, fish is cooked 10 minutes for every inch of thickness. For fillets, check for doneness by inserting a fork at an angle into the thickest portion of the fish and gently parting the meat. When it's opaque and flakes into sections, it is cooked completely.

Sliced peaches and red pepper strips add pretty color to these quick-to-fix pork slices, while a hint of Dijon mustard and gingerroot perks up the slightly sweet sauce.

**TERRI GLAUSER
APPLETON
WISCONSIN**

Pork Tenderloin Pointers: Keep pork tenderloin in the freezer for last-minute meals since it thaws and cooks quickly. Thaw using the "defrost" cycle of your microwave according to the manufacturer's directions.

peachy ginger pork

PREP/TOTAL TIME: 25 MIN.

1	pork tenderloin (1 pound), cut into 1/2-inch slices
1/2	teaspoon salt
1/8	teaspoon pepper
1	teaspoon olive oil
1	medium sweet red pepper, julienned
1	cup canned sliced peaches in extra-light syrup
1/2	cup chicken broth
1/3	cup peach spreadable fruit
1	tablespoon Dijon mustard
2	teaspoons minced fresh gingerroot

Flatten pork to 1/4-in. thickness; sprinkle with salt and pepper. In a large nonstick skillet coated with cooking spray, saute pork in oil in batches until juices run clear. Remove and keep warm.

In the same skillet, saute red pepper and peaches until the red pepper is tender. Add the broth, spreadable fruit, mustard and ginger. Cook and stir over medium heat for 4 minutes. Return pork to the pan. Reduce heat; cover and simmer until heated through. **Yield:** 4 servings.

monday's dish

TUESDAY WEDNESDAY THURSDAY FRIDAY

weekend prep reduces weekday rush...

Set aside some time on a Sunday to start doing meal prep for the week. After returning from the grocery store, wash any fresh vegetables, such as onions, celery and carrots. Then slice and dice according to this week's menu. Store in separate plastic containers or bags; refrigerate until you're ready to use them.

GROCERIES/

- [ ] 2 packages (10 ounces *each*) lemon-pepper marinated chicken breast fillets
- [ ] 1 pound ground beef
- [ ] 28 slices pepperoni
- [ ] 1 can (6 ounces) lump crabmeat
- [ ] 6 bone-in pork loin chops (about 3/4 inch thick and 7 ounces *each*)
- [ ] 2 medium green peppers
- [ ] 2 medium sweet red peppers
- [ ] 2 medium navel oranges
- [ ] 1 medium grapefruit
- [ ] 4 green onions
- [ ] 1 medium onion
- [ ] 1 package (3 ounces) shallots
- [ ] 1 bunch celery
- [ ] 4 cups mixed salad greens
- [ ] Fresh gingerroot
- [ ] 1 pound fresh asparagus
- [ ] 2 cups fresh snow peas
- [ ] 1 cup shredded carrots
- [ ] 1 can (8 ounces) pizza sauce
- [ ] 1/2 cup chopped pecans
- [ ] 1 can (3 ounces) chow mein noodles
- [ ] 1 can (14 ounces) coconut milk
- [ ] Rice vinegar
- [ ] Thai chili sauce
- [ ] 1 package (8.8 ounces) Asian rice noodles
- [ ] 1 can (8 ounces) sliced water chestnuts
- [ ] Sesame oil
- [ ] Dry roasted peanuts
- [ ] 6 flour tortillas (10 inches)
- [ ] 6 pieces (1 ounce *each*) string cheese

STAPLES/

- Barbecue sauce ▪ Butter
- Cayenne pepper ▪ Chili powder ▪ Cornstarch ▪ Creamy peanut butter ▪ Dried minced garlic ▪ Dried minced onion
- Dried oregano ▪ Dried thyme
- Ground cumin ▪ Lemon juice
- Mayonnaise ▪ Paprika
- Prepared horseradish
- Soy sauce ▪ Sugar

Store-bought packages of lemon-pepper chicken breasts speed assembly of this main dish. I usually prepare this when I want a fast and tasty meal.

GERTRUDIS MILLER
EVANSVILLE
INDIANA

Bread and Butter: Round out this skillet supper with fresh French bread and butter. Or bake refrigerated breadsticks or rolls.

20 lemon chicken and peppers

PREP/TOTAL TIME: 20 MIN.

2	packages (10 ounces *each*) lemon-pepper marinated chicken breast fillets
1/2	teaspoon paprika
1/4	teaspoon dried thyme
1	tablespoon butter
1	medium green pepper, cut into 1/4-inch strips
1	medium sweet red pepper, cut into 1/4-inch strips

Sprinkle chicken with paprika and thyme. In a large nonstick skillet, cook chicken in butter for 4-6 minutes on each side or until chicken juices run clear; drain and set aside. Saute peppers for 3-4 minutes or until tender. Return chicken to the pan; heat through. **Yield:** 4 servings.

This entree, a pizza-flavored roll-up, is sure to be popular with everyone at your table. They are easy to assemble.

TASTE OF HOME TEST KITCHEN

Ground Beef Basics: Look for ground beef that is bright red, avoiding any with brown or gray patches. The package should be tightly sealed, be free of tears and feel cold.

mozzarella beef roll-ups 30

PREP/TOTAL TIME: 30 MIN.

1	pound ground beef
1	medium green pepper, chopped
1/3	cup chopped onion
1	can (8 ounces) pizza sauce
28	slices pepperoni
1/2	teaspoon dried oregano
6	flour tortillas (10 inches), warmed
6	pieces (1 ounce *each*) string cheese

In a large skillet, cook the beef, green pepper and onion over medium heat until meat is no longer pink; drain. Stir in the pizza sauce, pepperoni and oregano.

Spoon about 1/2 cup beef mixture off-center on each tortilla; top with a piece of string cheese. Fold one side of tortilla over filling and roll up from the opposite side.

Place seam side down on an ungreased baking sheet. Bake at 350° for 10 minutes or until heated through and cheese is melted. **Yield:** 6 servings.

This salad is especially satisfying with oranges from our own trees.

**MARGARET PACHE
MESA, ARIZONA**

Cost-Saving Substitute: Imitation crabmeat, most often made with Alaskan pollack, can be substituted for real crab in equal proportions. But keep in mind that the flavor and texture will be different than the real thing.

orange crab salad

PREP/TOTAL TIME: 25 MIN.

2	medium navel oranges, peeled and sectioned
1	medium grapefruit, peeled and sectioned
4	green onions, chopped
1/2	cup chopped celery
1/2	cup chopped pecans
1	can (6 ounces) lump crabmeat, drained and flaked
4	cups mixed salad greens
1	can (3 ounces) chow mein noodles

GINGER SALAD DRESSING:

1/2	cup mayonnaise
2	teaspoons sugar
2	teaspoons lemon juice
2	teaspoons prepared horseradish
1	teaspoon minced fresh gingerroot

In a bowl, combine the first six ingredients. Divide the salad greens among four salad plates. Sprinkle with the chow mein noodles. Top each with about 3/4 cup crab mixture.

In a small bowl, whisk together the dressing ingredients. Serve with the crab salad. **Yield:** 4 servings.

These chops get their zesty appeal from a simple combination of herbs and seasonings.

**SANDY SHORT
CEDARVILLE, OHIO**

Greasing the Grill Rack: Spray the grate with cooking spray before starting the grill. Never spray directly over the fire (gas or coal). To grease a hot grate, fold a paper towel into a small pad. Holding the pad with long-handled tongs, dip in vegetable oil and rub over the grate.

southwest summer pork chops

PREP: 15 MIN. + MARINATING GRILL: 15 MIN.

4	teaspoons dried minced onion
2	teaspoons ground cumin
1	teaspoon cornstarch
1	teaspoon chili powder
1	teaspoon dried minced garlic
1/2	teaspoon dried oregano
1/2	teaspoon paprika
1/4	teaspoon cayenne pepper
6	bone-in pork loin chops (about 3/4 inch thick and 7 ounces *each*)
1/4	cup barbecue sauce
2	tablespoons lemon juice

In a small bowl, combine the first eight ingredients; rub over pork chops. In a large resealable plastic bag, combine barbecue sauce and lemon juice; add the pork chops; Seal the bag and turn to coat; refrigerate for 1-2 hours.

Discard marinade. If grilling the pork chops, coat grill rack with cooking spray before starting the grill. Grill chops, covered, over medium heat or broil 6 in. from the heat for 6-8 minutes on each side or until a meat thermometer reads 160°. **Yield:** 6 servings.

Take a pass on takeout! In no time at all, you can offer your family an entree inspired by the full-flavored foods of Thailand.

TASTE OF HOME TEST KITCHEN

Use Your Noodle: If you can't find Asian rice noodles in the Oriental cooking section of your grocery store, angel hair pasta or vermicelli can be used instead.

30) thai vegetable noodles

PREP/TOTAL TIME: 25 MIN.

2	teaspoons cornstarch
1/2	cup coconut milk
1/2	cup soy sauce
1/4	cup water
1/4	cup creamy peanut butter
2	tablespoons rice vinegar
5	teaspoons Thai chili sauce
1	tablespoon minced fresh gingerroot
4	ounces uncooked Asian rice noodles
1	pound fresh asparagus, trimmed and cut into 1-inch pieces
2	cups fresh snow peas
1	cup julienned sweet red pepper
1	cup shredded carrots
1	can (8 ounces) sliced water chestnuts, drained
1/4	cup chopped shallots
1	tablespoon sesame oil
1/4	cup chopped dry roasted peanuts

In a small bowl, combine the cornstarch, coconut milk, soy sauce, water, peanut butter, vinegar, chili sauce and ginger until blended; set aside.

Cook the noodles according to package directions. Meanwhile, in a large skillet, saute the asparagus, snow peas, red pepper, carrots, water chestnuts and shallots in oil for 5-8 minutes or until crisp-tender.

Stir soy sauce mixture and stir into skillet. Bring to a boil; cook and stir for 2 minutes or until thickened. Drain noodles; add to vegetable mixture and stir to coat. Sprinkle with peanuts. **Yield:** 4 servings.

friday's dish

MONDAY TUESDAY WEDNESDAY THURSDAY

GROCERIES/

- ☐ 4 bone-in pork loin chops (1 inch thick)
- ☐ 1 pound lean ground beef
- ☐ 1 pound uncooked large shrimp
- ☐ 1-1/2 pounds whitefish *or* cod fillets
- ☐ 1 pound smoked sausage
- ☐ 4 large apples
- ☐ 4 large green peppers
- ☐ Fresh parsley
- ☐ 1 large onion
- ☐ 1 package (15 ounces) golden raisins
- ☐ 1 can (14-1/2 ounces) diced tomatoes with mild green chilies
- ☐ 1 can (6 ounces) tomato paste
- ☐ Dry red wine
- ☐ 1 jar pimiento-stuffed olives
- ☐ Pistachios
- ☐ 1 can (16 ounces) kidney beans
- ☐ 1 package (24 ounces) frozen vegetable and pasta medley in garlic sauce
- ☐ Shredded Parmesan

STAPLES/

- Beef broth *or* beef bouillon
- Butter ▪ Cayenne pepper
- Cider vinegar ▪ Curry powder
- Dried basil ▪ Dried oregano
- Dried parsley flakes ▪ Dry bread crumbs ▪ Flour ▪ Garlic cloves ▪ Garlic powder
- Ground ginger ▪ Ground mustard ▪ Honey ▪ Lime juice
- Milk ▪ Oil (canola and olive)
- Pasta ▪ Pepper ▪ Rice ▪ Salt
- Seafood seasoning

tackle the dinner rush with fast foods...

From work and running errands to meetings and phone calls, you're often left wondering how you'll ever have time to fix dinner. All you need to beat the clock are family-favorite entrees that go from start to finish in 30 minutes or less. Each of these recipes has do-ahead elements, so you'll be able to get them on the table with time to spare!

When my husband and I lived in South Carolina for a year, some friends served this apple chutney. It became an instant favorite.

CHER ANJEMA
BRAMPTON
ONTARIO

Easy Chutney: Prepare the apple chutney a day ahead; let cool. Cover and chill. Reheat in a skillet over medium heat until warmed through. Serve with the chops.

30 > apple chutney chops

PREP/TOTAL TIME: 25 MIN.

4	cups chopped peeled apples
1/2	cup golden raisins
1/2	cup honey
3	tablespoons cider vinegar
1/2	teaspoon salt
1/2	teaspoon ground ginger
1/2	teaspoon ground mustard
1/2	teaspoon curry powder
4	bone-in pork loin chops (1 inch thick)
1	tablespoon canola oil

For chutney, in a large saucepan, combine the apples, raisins, honey, vinegar, salt, ginger, mustard and curry. Bring to a boil. Reduce heat; simmer, uncovered, for 10-15 minutes or until apples are tender.

Meanwhile, in a large skillet, brown the pork chops in oil over medium-high heat for 2-3 minutes on each side. Reduce heat; cook, uncovered, for 10-15 minutes or until juices run clear. Serve with apple chutney. **Yield:** 4 servings.

Cooking green pepper halves in the microwave really cuts down the cooking time.

TASTE OF HOME TEST KITCHEN

Simple Stuffed Peppers: The night before, clean, seed and cut the peppers; refrigerate in a resealable plastic bag. Make the ground beef; cover and chill. The next day, reheat the filling before stuffing the peppers.

cuban-style stuffed peppers 30〉

PREP/TOTAL TIME: 25 MIN.

1	pound lean ground beef
1/2	cup chopped onion
2	teaspoons minced garlic
2	teaspoons olive oil
1	can (14-1/2 ounces) diced tomatoes with mild green chilies
1	cup cooked long grain rice
1/4	cup dry red wine
1/4	cup sliced pimiento-stuffed olives
3	tablespoons tomato paste
2	teaspoons dried oregano
1	teaspoon salt
1/2	teaspoon pepper
4	large green peppers
1	cup water

Roasted sweet red pepper strips, optional

In a large skillet, cook beef, onion and garlic in oil over medium heat until meat is no longer pink; drain. Stir in the next eight ingredients. Bring to a boil. Reduce heat; simmer, uncovered, for 15-20 minutes.

Meanwhile, cut the green peppers in half lengthwise; discard seeds. Place in an ungreased shallow 3-qt. microwave-safe dish; add water. Cover and microwave on high for 8-10 minutes or until crisp-tender. Drain; fill each pepper half with 1/2 cup meat mixture. Garnish with red pepper strips if desired. **Yield:** 4 servings.

EDITOR'S NOTE: This recipe was tested in a 1,100-watt microwave.

Our son, a restaurant owner, showed me how to make this quick shrimp and noodle dish zipped up with garlic and cayenne. It's also tasty served over rice.

GERTRAUD CASBARRO
SUMMERVILLE
SOUTH CAROLINA

20) garlic lime shrimp

PREP/TOTAL TIME: 20 MIN.

1	pound uncooked large shrimp, peeled and deveined
5	garlic cloves, minced
1/2	teaspoon salt
1/4	to 1/2 teaspoon cayenne pepper
1/2	cup butter
3	tablespoons lime juice
1	tablespoon minced fresh parsley

Hot cooked pasta

In a large skillet, saute the shrimp, garlic, salt and cayenne in butter until the shrimp turn pink, about 5 minutes. Stir in lime juice and parsley. Serve with the pasta. **Yield:** 4 servings.

DO-AHEAD TASK: (tip)

Peel and devein the shrimp the night before. Place in a resealable plastic bag and chill. Or pick up peeled and deveined shrimp from the supermarket.

This nut-crusted fish is so much better than ordinary breaded fish. Pistachios give it great color.

**TASTE OF HOME
TEST KITCHEN**

 Quick Coating: A few days before, assemble the pistachio coating by combining the first six ingredients. Store at room temperature in an airtight container.

pistachio-crusted fried fish 30〉

PREP/TOTAL TIME: 30 MIN.

1/2	cup dry bread crumbs
1/2	cup chopped pistachios
1/2	teaspoon seafood seasoning
1/4	teaspoon salt
1/4	teaspoon garlic powder
1/4	teaspoon pepper
1/2	cup all-purpose flour
1/2	cup milk
1-1/2	pounds whitefish *or* cod fillets
3	tablespoons canola oil

In a shallow bowl, combine the first six ingredients. Place flour and milk in separate shallow bowls. Dip fillets in flour, then in milk; coat with pistachio mixture.

In a large nonstick skillet, cook fillets in oil over medium heat for 4-5 minutes on each side or until fish flakes easily with a fork. **Yield:** 6 servings.

I maximize the potential of convenience products to create a hearty soup for cold winter nights. This full-bodied dish contains lots of beans, veggies and sausage.

**DONA HOFFMAN
ADDISON
ILLINOIS**

Fast from the Freezer: Speedy Minestrone lives up to its name! But to save even more time, keep a package of frozen chopped onions in the freezer. Instead of cutting up a fresh onion, measure out how much chopped onion you need from the bag.

30 > speedy minestrone

PREP/TOTAL TIME: 25 MIN.

2 cans (14-1/2 ounces *each*) beef broth
1 package (24 ounces) frozen vegetable and pasta medley in garlic sauce
1 pound smoked sausage, cut into 1/2-inch slices
1 can (16 ounces) kidney beans, rinsed and drained
1/4 cup chopped onion
1 teaspoon dried basil
1 teaspoon dried parsley flakes
Shredded Parmesan cheese

In a large saucepan, combine the first seven ingredients. Bring to a boil. Reduce heat; simmer, uncovered, for 10-15 minutes or until heated through. Sprinkle with the Parmesan cheese. **Yield:** 6 servings.

tuesday's dish

MONDAY WEDNESDAY THURSDAY FRIDAY

GROCERIES/

- ☐ 1 pound boneless beef sirloin steak
- ☐ 6 orange roughy fillets (6 ounces each)
- ☐ 1/2 pound smoked sausage
- ☐ 2 cups shredded cooked turkey breast
- ☐ Fresh gingerroot
- ☐ 1/2 pound fresh broccoli
- ☐ 2 medium sweet red peppers
- ☐ 2 medium carrots
- ☐ 1 small onion
- ☐ 1 small red onion
- ☐ 4 green onions
- ☐ 1 medium cucumber
- ☐ 1 yellow summer squash
- ☐ 2 plum tomatoes
- ☐ 1/2 pound sliced fresh mushrooms
- ☐ 1 small zucchini
- ☐ 1 head lettuce
- ☐ 2 medium ripe avocados
- ☐ 1 pound (about 3 medium) tomatoes
- ☐ 1 jar (7 ounces) plum sauce
- ☐ Salted peanuts
- ☐ 1 jar (16 ounces) chunky salsa
- ☐ 1 can (11 ounces) shoepeg corn
- ☐ 1 can (16 ounces) vegetarian refried beans
- ☐ 8 ounces spaghetti
- ☐ 1 can (12 ounces) evaporated milk
- ☐ 1 prebaked thin Italian bread shell crust (10 ounces)
- ☐ 1 jar (17 ounces) Alfredo sauce
- ☐ 1 package (9 ounces) frozen broccoli cuts
- ☐ 1 package (10 ounces) frozen chopped spinach
- ☐ 6 flour tortillas (8 inches)
- ☐ 1-1/2 cups (6 ounces) shredded cheddar cheese
- ☐ 1 carton (8 ounces) sour cream
- ☐ Shredded Parmesan

STAPLES/

- Butter Cornstarch
- Crushed red pepper flakes
- Garlic cloves Grated Parmesan cheese Italian seasoning Lemon juice
- Lemon-pepper seasoning
- Lime juice Oil (canola and olive) Pepper Rice Salt
- Sesame seeds Soy sauce

weeknight entertaining made easy...

It's hard to say who will be more impressed by this weeknight dinner plan: your family when they sit down to scrumptious meals like these every night...or you when meal prep is wrapped up in record time! For perfect endings to these delectable dinners, check out the delicious dessert options starting on page 193. Don't forget to shop ahead for those treats, too!

This quick stir-fry is so colorful and tasty. To save even more time, I sometimes pick up prepared veggies from our grocery store's salad bar.

**LINDA MURRAY
ALLENSTOWN
NEW HAMPSHIRE**

Taste Twist: You can vary this recipe by substituting chicken or other vegetables you have on hand.

30 > ginger beef stir-fry
PREP/TOTAL TIME: 30 MIN.

- 1 teaspoon cornstarch
- 1/4 cup cold water
- 1/4 cup plum sauce
- 1 tablespoon grated fresh gingerroot
- 1 tablespoon soy sauce
- 1/4 teaspoon crushed red pepper flakes
- 1 pound boneless beef sirloin steak, cut into thin 2-inch strips
- 1 to 2 tablespoons canola oil
- 1 medium sweet red pepper, julienned
- 1-1/2 cups fresh broccoli florets
- 2 medium carrots, thinly sliced
- 4 green onions, chopped
- 1 teaspoon minced garlic
- 3 tablespoons salted peanuts, chopped

Hot cooked rice, optional
- 2 tablespoons sesame seeds, toasted

In a small bowl, whisk cornstarch and cold water until smooth. Stir in the plum sauce, ginger, soy sauce and pepper flakes; set aside. In a large skillet or wok, stir-fry beef in oil until no longer pink; remove and keep warm.

In the same pan, stir-fry the red pepper, broccoli, carrots, onions and garlic until tender. Return beef to the pan. Whisk the plum sauce mixture; stir into skillet.

Cook and stir until slightly thickened. Stir in peanuts. Serve with rice if desired. Sprinkle with sesame seeds. **Yield:** 4 servings.

Topped with a healthy dollop of cool and colorful Cucumber Salsa, orange roughy makes a light and lovely entree that goes together in minutes.

TASTE OF HOME TEST KITCHEN

Fish Facts: Orange roughy is an all-purpose white-fleshed fish. Any whitefish fillets (like ocean perch, cod and haddock) can be substituted in its place.

basil walnut fettuccine, pg. 185

orange roughy 20⟩
with cucumber salsa

PREP/TOTAL TIME: 20 MIN.

1	cup chopped cucumber
1/2	cup chopped yellow summer squash
2	plum tomatoes, chopped
1/4	cup chopped red onion
1	tablespoon lime juice
2	teaspoons olive oil
1/4	teaspoon salt
2	teaspoons lemon-pepper seasoning
6	orange roughy fillets (6 ounces each)

For salsa, in a small bowl, combine the first seven ingredients; set aside. Sprinkle lemon-pepper over both sides of fillets.

Place on a broiler pan coated with cooking spray. Broil 4-6 in. from the heat for 3-4 minutes on each side or until fish flakes easily with a fork. Serve with cucumber salsa. **Yield:** 6 servings.

Your family won't miss the meat in tasty tostadas topped with refried beans, corn, zucchini and salsa.

TASTE OF HOME TEST KITCHEN

Try Tostada Shells: (tip) Instead of using flour tortillas, pick up a pack of crisp tostada shells. Or turn this dish into a hearty salad by tossing in more lettuce and using store-bought taco-salad shells.

30 ⟩ refried bean tostadas

PREP/TOTAL TIME: 30 MIN.

6	flour tortillas (8 inches)
1/2	pound sliced fresh mushrooms
1	cup diced zucchini
2	tablespoons canola oil
1	jar (16 ounces) chunky salsa
1	can (11 ounces) shoepeg corn, drained
1	can (16 ounces) vegetarian refried beans, warmed
1-1/2	cups shredded lettuce
1-1/2	cups (6 ounces) shredded cheddar cheese
2	medium ripe avocados, peeled and sliced
1-1/2	cups chopped tomatoes
6	tablespoons sour cream

In a large ungreased skillet, cook tortillas for 1-2 minutes on each side or until lightly browned. Remove and set aside.

In the same skillet, saute mushrooms and zucchini in oil until crisp-tender. Add salsa and corn; cook for 2-3 minutes or until heated through.

Spread refried beans over each tortilla; top with lettuce, salsa mixture, cheese, avocados, tomatoes and sour cream. **Yield:** 6 servings.

My family loves Italian food, and this delicious, creamy sauce is a nice change of pace from tomato-based dishes.

MISTY CHURCH
ST. PETERSBURG
FLORIDA

Leftover Milk: One 12-ounce can of evaporated milk is equal to 1-1/2 cups. This recipe calls for 3/4 cup. Use the leftover milk in place of half-and-half cream in your coffee.

smoked sausage primavera 30

PREP/TOTAL TIME: 25 MIN.

8	ounces uncooked spaghetti
1-1/2	cups frozen broccoli cuts
1/2	cup julienned sweet red, yellow *and/or* green pepper
1/4	cup coarsely chopped onion
1/2	pound smoked sausage, cut into 1/2-inch slices
1/4	cup water
3/4	cup evaporated milk
2	tablespoons butter
1/2	teaspoon Italian seasoning
1/4	cup grated Parmesan cheese

In a Dutch oven, cook spaghetti according to package directions, adding broccoli, pepper and onion during the last 4 minutes.

Meanwhile, in a large skillet, bring sausage and water to a boil. Reduce heat; cover and simmer for 7-8 minutes or until heated through. Add the milk, butter and Italian seasoning; cook and stir until the butter is melted.

Drain spaghetti and vegetables; return to the pan. Add cheese and sausage mixture; toss to coat. **Yield:** 4 servings.

A long-time family favorite, this thin-crusted pizza is chock-full of flavor and nutrition—and an excellent way to use up leftover turkey.

EDIE DESPAIN
LOGAN, UTAH

Pizza for One:  Make individual pizzas by using 2 packages (10 ounces each) prebaked mini Italian bread shell crusts.

30 > turkey alfredo pizza

PREP/TOTAL TIME: 25 MIN.

1	prebaked thin Italian bread shell crust (10 ounces)
1	garlic clove, peeled and halved
3/4	cup Alfredo sauce, *divided*
1	package (10 ounces) frozen chopped spinach, thawed and squeezed dry
2	teaspoons lemon juice
1/4	teaspoon salt
1/8	teaspoon pepper
2	cups shredded cooked turkey breast
3/4	cup shredded Parmesan cheese
1/2	teaspoon crushed red pepper flakes

Place the crust on a baking sheet; rub with cut sides of garlic. Discard garlic. Spread 1/2 cup Alfredo sauce over crust.

In a small bowl, combine the spinach, lemon juice, salt and pepper; spoon evenly over sauce. Top with the turkey; drizzle with remaining Alfredo sauce. Sprinkle with Parmesan cheese and pepper flakes.

Bake at 425° for 11-13 minutes or until heated through and cheese is melted. **Yield:** 6 servings.

friday's dish

MONDAY   TUESDAY   WEDNESDAY   THURSDAY

GROCERIES/

- ☐ 4 tilapia fillets (6 ounces *each*)
- ☐ 3 cups cubed cooked chicken
- ☐ 1 pound boneless beef sirloin steak
- ☐ 4 bone-in pork loin chops (3/4 inch thick and 8 ounces *each*)
- ☐ 1 pound ground beef
- ☐ 3 small red potatoes
- ☐ 1 cup cherry tomatoes
- ☐ 1 cup pineapple chunks
- ☐ 1 medium sweet orange pepper
- ☐ 1 medium green pepper
- ☐ 1/4 pound sliced fresh mushrooms
- ☐ 1 jar (3-1/2 ounces) capers
- ☐ 1 can (10-3/4 ounces) condensed cream of chicken soup
- ☐ 1 jar (4-1/2 ounces) sliced mushrooms
- ☐ 1 can cola
- ☐ 1 can (8 ounces) tomato sauce
- ☐ 1 tube (12 ounces) refrigerated buttermilk biscuits
- ☐ 4 slices part-skim mozzarella cheese

STAPLES/

■ Butter ■ Chicken broth *or* chicken bouillon ■ Dill weed ■ Dried basil ■ Dried minced onion ■ Dried oregano ■ Dried parsley flakes ■ Egg ■ Flour ■ Garlic cloves ■ Garlic powder ■ Grated Parmesan cheese ■ Italian seasoning ■ Ketchup ■ Lemon juice ■ Milk ■ Oil (canola and olive) ■ Paprika ■ Pasta (gemelli *or* spiral) ■ Pepper ■ Salt ■ Soft bread crumbs ■ Steak seasoning ■ Worcestershire sauce

meals appeal to kids of all ages...

Weekday dinners are a terrific time to introduce young diners to fabulous new flavors. While grown-ups at the table will fall for this week's succulent selections, children will also love the great-tasting feast. Sneak in even more nourishing nutrients by offering any of these entrees with chilled fresh fruit, which will also satisfy after-supper sweet tooths!

I've decided to cook healthier for my family, and that includes having more fish at home. This is a great recipe, and it's fast, too!

HOPE STEWART
RALEIGH
NORTH CAROLINA

20 baked tilapia

PREP/TOTAL TIME: 20 MIN.

4	tilapia fillets (6 ounces *each*)
3	tablespoons butter, melted
3	tablespoons lemon juice
1-1/2	teaspoons garlic powder
1/8	teaspoon salt
2	tablespoons capers, drained
1/2	teaspoon dried oregano
1/8	teaspoon paprika

LEMON OR LIME? (tip)

Lemon and lime juice can be used interchangeably in equal amounts in most recipes. Add a little of both for a refreshing lemon-lime flavor.

Place tilapia in an ungreased 13-in. x 9-in. baking dish. In a small bowl, combine the butter, lemon juice, garlic powder and salt; pour over the fillets. Sprinkle with capers, oregano and paprika.

Bake, uncovered, at 425° for 10-15 minutes or until the fish flakes easily with a fork. **Yield:** 4 servings.

Topped with seasoned golden biscuits, this yummy casserole will fill up a family.

KAYLA DEMPSEY
O'FALLON, ILLINOIS

Sunday Chicken Dinner: Some Sunday, roast two chickens for a down-home dinner. Enjoy one, then remove the meat from the other bird; cut into cubes. Freeze in 1-cup measures in heavy-duty resealable plastic bags to use in weekday casseroles.

biscuit nugget chicken bake 30

PREP/TOTAL TIME: 30 MIN.

3   cups cubed cooked chicken
1   can (10-3/4 ounces) condensed cream of chicken soup, undiluted
1   cup milk
1   jar (4-1/2 ounces) sliced mushrooms, drained
1/2 teaspoon dill weed
1/2 teaspoon paprika
TOPPING:
1/4 cup grated Parmesan cheese
1   tablespoon dried minced onion
1   teaspoon dried parsley flakes
1/2 teaspoon paprika
1   tube (12 ounces) refrigerated buttermilk biscuits

In a large saucepan, combine the first six ingredients. Cook and stir over medium heat for 5-7 minutes or until heated through; keep warm.

In a large resealable plastic bag, combine the Parmesan cheese, onion, parsley and paprika. Separate biscuits and cut into quarters; add to bag and shake to coat. Place on an ungreased baking sheet. Bake at 400° for 5 minutes.

Transfer chicken mixture to a greased 8-in. square baking dish; top with biscuits. Bake, uncovered, for 10-13 minutes or until bubbly and the biscuits are golden brown. **Yield:** 4-6 servings.

You'll love this quick recipe. The potatoes are cooked in the microwave first, so grilling is super-easy.

TASTE OF HOME TEST KITCHEN

Soak Your Skewers: If using wooden skewers for kabobs, be sure to soak them in cold water for at least 15 minutes. This will prevent them from burning on the grill.

parmesan couscous, pg. 177

30 meat 'n' potato kabobs

PREP/TOTAL TIME: 30 MIN.

1	pound boneless beef sirloin steak, cut into 1-inch cubes
1-1/2	teaspoons steak seasoning, *divided*
1	teaspoon minced garlic
1	cup cola
3	small red potatoes, cubed
1	tablespoon water
1	cup cherry tomatoes
1	medium sweet orange pepper, cut into 1-inch pieces
1	teaspoon canola oil
1	cup pineapple chunks

Sprinkle beef cubes with 1 teaspoon steak seasoning and garlic; place in a large resealable plastic bag. Add cola. Seal bag and turn to coat; set aside.

Place the potatoes and the water in a microwave-safe dish; cover and microwave on high for 4 minutes or until tender. Drain. Add the tomatoes, orange pepper, oil and the remaining steak seasoning; toss gently to coat.

Drain and discard marinade. Alternately thread the beef, vegetables and pineapple onto eight metal or soaked wooden skewers. Grill, covered, over medium-hot heat or broil 4-6 in. from the heat for 4 minutes on each side or until meat reaches desired doneness (for medium-rare, a meat thermometer should read 145°; medium, 160°; well-done, 170°). **Yield:** 4 servings.

EDITOR'S NOTE: This recipe was tested in a 1,100-watt microwave and was tested with McCormick's Montreal Steak Seasoning. Look for it in the spice aisle.

These juicy chops are covered with a basil-seasoned tomato sauce and melted cheese. Children as well as adults love them.

JANENE
CHRISTENSEN
EUREKA, MISSOURI

Make It Mexican! To give these chops Southwestern-style flair, replace the tomato sauce, water, Italian seasoning and basil with salsa. Use Monterey Jack cheese instead of mozzarella.

pork chops italiano 30>

PREP/TOTAL TIME: 25 MIN.

4	bone-in pork loin chops (3/4 inch thick and 8 ounces *each*)
1/4	teaspoon pepper
2	tablespoons butter
1	can (8 ounces) tomato sauce
1/4	cup water
1	teaspoon Italian seasoning
1/2	teaspoon dried basil
4	slices part-skim mozzarella cheese
1	medium green pepper, cut into rings

Sprinkle pork chops with pepper. In a large skillet, brown chops in butter on both sides; drain. Combine the tomato sauce, water, Italian seasoning and basil; pour over chops. Bring to a boil. Reduce heat; cover and simmer for 6-8 minutes or until meat juices run clear.

Top each pork chop with cheese and green pepper. Cover and cook 3-5 minutes longer or until cheese is melted. **Yield:** 4 servings.

This streamlined classic has great flavor and appeal. It's a crowd-pleaser ideal for busy weeknights.

TASTE OF HOME TEST KITCHEN

Freezing Ground Beef: Ground beef is a great ingredient to have on hand for fast meals. Place uncooked ground beef in a heavy-duty resealable plastic bag; freeze and use within 3 months.

30 salisbury steak with gemelli

PREP/TOTAL TIME: 30 MIN.

1 egg
1/2 cup soft bread crumbs
1 teaspoon Italian seasoning
1/2 teaspoon pepper
1/2 teaspoon minced garlic
1 pound ground beef
1 tablespoon olive oil
1 cup sliced fresh mushrooms
2 tablespoons all-purpose flour
1 cup chicken broth
1 tablespoon ketchup
1 teaspoon Worcestershire sauce
Hot cooked gemelli *or* spiral pasta

In a large bowl, combine the egg, bread crumbs, Italian seasoning, pepper and garlic. Crumble beef over mixture and mix well. Shape into four patties.

In a large skillet, cook patties in oil over medium-high heat for 5-7 minutes on each side or until meat is no longer pink. Remove and keep warm.

Drain, reserving 2 tablespoons drippings. Saute mushrooms in drippings until tender. Stir in flour until blended. Gradually stir in the broth, ketchup and Worcestershire sauce. Bring to a boil; cook and stir for 2 minutes or until thickened.

Return patties to the skillet. Bring to a boil. Reduce heat; simmer, uncovered, for 3-4 minutes or until heated through. Serve with gemelli. **Yield:** 4 servings.

thursday's dish

MONDAY TUESDAY WEDNESDAY FRIDAY

GROCERIES/

- ☐ 4 boneless skinless chicken breast halves (6 ounces *each*)
- ☐ 4 boneless beef top loin steaks (8 ounces *each*)
- ☐ 2 boneless pork loin chops (1/2 inch thick and 4 ounces *each*)
- ☐ 1/4 pound thinly sliced cooked turkey
- ☐ 2 medium yellow summer squash
- ☐ 2 medium zucchini
- ☐ 1 pint cherry tomatoes
- ☐ 1 medium onion
- ☐ 4 green onions
- ☐ 2 jars (7 ounces *each*) roasted sweet red peppers
- ☐ Sliced almonds
- ☐ 1 can (7 ounces) chipotle peppers in adobo sauce
- ☐ 1 bottle creamy Caesar salad dressing
- ☐ 1 bottle honey Dijon salad dressing
- ☐ 4 ounces crumbled feta cheese
- ☐ 1 carton (8 ounces) sour cream
- ☐ 1 package (9 ounces) refrigerated cheese tortellini
- ☐ Shredded Parmesan
- ☐ 4 slices Monterey Jack cheese
- ☐ 4 slices whole wheat bread

STAPLES/

- ▪ Brown sugar ▪ Butter ▪ Chili powder ▪ Dried cilantro flakes
- ▪ Dry bread crumbs ▪ Egg
- ▪ Flour ▪ Garlic powder
- ▪ Italian seasoning
- ▪ Mayonnaise ▪ Olive oil
- ▪ Pepper ▪ Prepared mustard
- ▪ Salt

easy meals mean less time in the kitchen...

Time with your loved ones is often limited on busy weekdays. No cooks want to spend precious moments in the kitchen preparing complicated meals when they could be sitting around the table reconnecting with their families. All of this week's recipes go from start to finish in 25 minutes or less. So there's plenty of time to eat and to catch up!

This lightly breaded, moist and tender chicken is cooked to perfection.

TASTE OF HOME TEST KITCHEN

Feta Facts:
Feta is a white, salty, semi-firm cheese. Traditionally, it was made from sheep or goat's milk but is now also prepared from cow's milk.

30 chicken with red pepper sauce

PREP/TOTAL TIME: 25 MIN.

1	egg
1/2	cup dry bread crumbs
1/4	teaspoon salt
4	boneless skinless chicken breast halves (6 ounces *each*)
2	tablespoons olive oil
2	jars (7 ounces *each*) roasted sweet red peppers, drained
1	teaspoon Italian seasoning
3/4	cup crumbled feta cheese

In a shallow bowl, lightly beat the egg. In another shallow bowl, combine bread crumbs and salt. Dip chicken in egg, then coat with the crumbs.

In a large skillet, cook chicken in oil over medium heat for 6-8 minutes on each side or until juices run clear.

Meanwhile, in a blender or food processor, combine the red peppers and Italian seasoning; cover and process until pureed. Transfer to a microwave-safe bowl. Cover and microwave on high for 1-2 minutes or until heated through, stirring once. Spoon over chicken; sprinkle with feta cheese. **Yield:** 4 servings.

Chipotles in adobo sauce are dried smoked red jalapeno peppers, which are canned with a thick chili puree called adobo.
TASTE OF HOME TEST KITCHEN

 Save Leftover Peppers: Unused chipotle peppers can be frozen. Individually freeze the peppers with some sauce on a lined baking sheet, then store in a resealable plastic freezer bag for up to 3 months.

steaks with chipotle sauce

PREP/TOTAL TIME: 25 MIN.

1	can (7 ounces) chipotle peppers in adobo sauce
1/2	cup sour cream
1	teaspoon dried cilantro flakes
4	boneless beef top loin steaks (8 ounces *each*)

Chop one chipotle pepper; place in a bowl. Add 1 teaspoon of the adobo sauce. Stir in the sour cream and cilantro; refrigerate. (Save the remaining peppers and sauce for another use.)

Grill steaks, uncovered, over medium-hot heat for 6-10 minutes on each side or until the meat reaches desired doneness (for medium-rare, a meat thermometer should read 145°; medium, 160°; well-done, 170°). Serve with sauce. **Yield:** 4 servings.

EDITOR'S NOTE: Top loin steak may be labeled as strip steak, Kansas City steak, New York strip steak, ambassador steak or boneless club steak in your region.

This meal-in-one calls for just a few ingredients, including refrigerated store-bought pasta.

MARY ANN DELL
PHOENIXVILLE
PENNSYLVANIA

Cutting Green Onions:

It's easier and faster to cut green onions with a kitchen scissors than with a knife. If the recipe calls for quite a few, grab a bunch at one time and snip away.

 tortellini primavera

PREP/TOTAL TIME: 20 MIN.

- 1 package (9 ounces) refrigerated cheese tortellini
- 2 medium yellow summer squash, chopped
- 2 medium zucchini, chopped
- 2 teaspoons olive oil
- 1 pint cherry tomatoes, halved
- 1/2 cup chopped green onions
- 1/4 teaspoon pepper
- 1/2 cup creamy Caesar salad dressing
- 1/4 cup shredded Parmesan cheese
- 1/4 cup sliced almonds, toasted

Cook tortellini according to package directions. Meanwhile, in a large skillet, saute yellow squash and zucchini in oil for 4-6 minutes or until crisp-tender.

Drain tortellini; place in a large bowl. Add the squash mixture, tomatoes, onions and pepper. Drizzle with salad dressing; toss to coat. Sprinkle with Parmesan cheese and almonds. **Yield:** 6 servings.

> My husband used to get home from work before me, and one evening, he cooked this for dinner. We've depended on the same recipe ever since. It's delicious.
>
> **KATHY KIRKLAND
> DENHAM SPRINGS
> LOUISIANA**

festive corn 'n' broccoli, pg. 177

sweet 'n' spicy pork chops [20]

PREP/TOTAL TIME: 20 MIN.

2   boneless pork loin chops (1/2 inch thick and 4 ounces *each*)

Dash salt and pepper

2   tablespoons brown sugar
1   tablespoon finely chopped onion
1   to 1-1/2 teaspoons chili powder
1/2   teaspoon garlic powder
1/2   teaspoon prepared mustard

Sprinkle both sides of pork chops with salt and pepper. Place on a rack in a foil-lined broiler pan. Broil chops 4 in. from the heat for 5 minutes.

Combine the remaining ingredients. Turn chops; spread with brown sugar mixture. Broil 5-8 minutes longer or until juices run clear. **Yield:** 2 servings.

LIGHT VERSUS DARK

Both light and dark brown sugars are a mixture of granulated sugars and molasses, with dark brown sugar containing more molasses than light brown sugar. Light brown sugar has a delicate flavor while dark brown sugar has a stronger, more intense molasses taste. They can be used interchangeably depending on your personal preference.

I enjoy making this when I am craving comfort food but don't have the time or energy for a big meal. It works well with deli or leftover turkey.

**SARAH MARSHALL
CREEDMOOR
NORTH CAROLINA**

Eat Your Veggies: Keep carrot and celery sticks on hand for a fast side dish. Clean and slice the vegetables as soon as you come home from the store. Place in a covered container and refrigerate in the crisper for up to 2 weeks.

30⟩ turkey dijon melts

PREP/TOTAL TIME: 25 MIN.

4	slices whole wheat bread
4	teaspoons mayonnaise
1/4	pound thinly sliced cooked turkey
4	slices Monterey Jack cheese
1/4	cup thinly sliced onion

Dash salt and pepper

1	tablespoon honey Dijon salad dressing
1	tablespoon butter, softened

Spread two slices of bread with mayonnaise. Layer with turkey, cheese and onion; sprinkle with salt and pepper. Spread remaining slices of bread with salad dressing; place over onion. Butter outsides of sandwiches.

In a small skillet over medium heat, toast sandwiches for 4-5 minutes on each side or until bread is lightly browned and cheese is melted. **Yield:** 2 servings.

thursday's dish

MONDAY TUESDAY WEDNESDAY FRIDAY

GROCERIES/

- ☐ 16 slices Canadian bacon
- ☐ 1-1/2 pounds ground beef
- ☐ 1 pound boneless pork loin
- ☐ 1 pound chicken tenderloins
- ☐ 2 medium green peppers
- ☐ 1 medium onion
- ☐ 4 green onions
- ☐ 1 medium leek
- ☐ 1 bunch celery
- ☐ 1 head lettuce
- ☐ 2 large tomatoes
- ☐ 1 medium head cabbage
- ☐ 1 pound fresh baby carrots
- ☐ 1 package (8 ounces) fresh sugar snap peas
- ☐ 1 jar marinara sauce
- ☐ 1 can (20 ounces) unsweetened pineapple tidbits
- ☐ 1 can (10 ounces) diced tomatoes and green chilies
- ☐ 1 can (29 ounces) tomato puree
- ☐ 1 can (14-1/2 ounces) diced tomatoes
- ☐ 1 package (16 ounces) frozen lima beans
- ☐ 1 package (10 ounces) frozen puff pastry shells
- ☐ 2 cups (8 ounces) shredded part-skim mozzarella cheese
- ☐ 1 pound process cheese (Velveeta)
- ☐ Egg substitute
- ☐ 1 bag corn chips
- ☐ 1 loaf (1 pound) French bread

STAPLES/

- Bay leaves ▪ Butter ▪ Canola oil ▪ Chili powder ▪ Dried basil ▪ Dried oregano ▪ Dry bread crumbs ▪ Garlic cloves ▪ Ground cumin ▪ Paprika ▪ Pepper ▪ Prepared mustard ▪ Salt ▪ Sugar

shopping shortcuts round out dinners...

The main dish is the most important part of the meal...and often the course you want to prepare from scratch. Round out these homemade recipes with meal helpers from the grocery store. Grab a bag of mixed greens for a simple side salad. Or stop by the bakery for a fresh loaf of bread to serve alongside the meal.

Canadian bacon with pineapple and green pepper on French bread makes a quick pizza.

TASTE OF HOME TEST KITCHEN

Canadian Bacon Basics: Canadian bacon (known as back bacon in Canada) comes from the eye of the loin in the middle of the back of the animal. It's not really bacon, because it's much leaner and the flavor and consistency of ham. Use Canadian bacon as you would ham, rather than as bacon.

30⟩ canadian bacon pizza

PREP/TOTAL TIME: 25 MIN.

1	loaf (1 pound) French bread
1/4	cup butter, melted
2	cups marinara sauce
16	slices Canadian bacon
1	can (20 ounces) unsweetened pineapple tidbits, drained
1/2	cup chopped green pepper
1/4	cup chopped green onions
2	cups (8 ounces) shredded part-skim mozzarella cheese

Cut bread in half lengthwise, then in half widthwise. Place cut side up in a foil-lined 15-in. x 10-in. x 1-in. baking pan. Brush with butter. Bake at 450° for 5 minutes or until lightly browned.

Spread marinara sauce over bread. Top with Canadian bacon, pineapple, green pepper, onions and cheese. Bake for 8-10 minutes or until cheese is melted. Cut each piece in half. **Yield:** 8 servings.

My family gobbles up this spicy salad. So I often double the recipe to have leftovers for lunch the next day.

ARLENE GHENT
ST. JOSEPH
MISSOURI

Versatile Filling: The beef filling can also be used with flour tortillas to make soft-shell tacos or burritos. Or roll up the flour tortillas, top with a can of enchilada sauce and bake for easy enchiladas.

cheesy beef taco salad 30

PREP/TOTAL TIME: 30 MIN.

1-1/2 pounds ground beef
1-1/2 cups chopped onion
1 cup diced celery
1 cup diced green pepper
2 garlic cloves, minced
1 pound process cheese (Velveeta), cubed
1 can (10 ounces) diced tomatoes and green chilies, undrained
2 teaspoons chili powder
2 teaspoons ground cumin
1-1/2 cups crushed corn chips
Shredded lettuce
Chopped green onions
2 large tomatoes, cut into wedges

In a large skillet, cook the beef, onion, celery, green pepper and garlic over medium heat until meat is no longer pink; drain. Stir in the cheese, tomatoes, chili powder and cumin. Cook and stir over low heat until cheese is melted. Stir in corn chips.

Line six salad plates with lettuce; sprinkle with the green onions. Top each with 1 cup of the beef mixture. Garnish with tomato wedges. **Yield:** 6 servings.

For a one-pan dinner that's fast and easy, I mildly season pork slices and cabbage strips. A side of rice completes the meal.

ROSEMARY GISIN
PEEKSKILL, NEW YORK

30› pork cabbage saute

PREP/TOTAL TIME: 25 MIN.

1	pound boneless pork loin, cut into 2-inch strips
1	tablespoon canola oil
1/2	medium head cabbage, shredded
1	medium onion, thinly sliced
1/2	teaspoon minced garlic
2	bay leaves
2	tablespoons butter
1/2	teaspoon salt
1/2	teaspoon pepper

In a large skillet, cook and stir the pork in oil over medium heat until no longer pink; remove the keep warm. In the same skillet, saute the cabbage, onion, garlic and bay leaves in butter until vegetables are tender. Discard bay leaves. Stir in pork, salt and pepper. **Yield:** 4 servings.

BASICS OF BUYING CABBAGE (tip)

Buy round, compact solid heads of cabbage. The leaves should be tight, smooth and unblemished. Place unwashed cabbage in a sealed plastic bag in the refrigerator crisper drawer for 1 to 2 weeks. Wash before using. Remove any discolored or damaged leaves.

These strips are designed for kids, but tasty enough for company. They're moist and juicy and would also be great on a salad.

BECKY OLIVER
FAIRPLAY, COLORADO

Simple Side Dish: Mashed potatoes make a great side dish for any kind of chicken. If you don't have time to make them from scratch, pick up a bag of refrigerated mashed potatoes and cook as directed.

seasoned chicken strips

PREP/TOTAL TIME: 25 MIN.

1/3	cup egg substitute
1	tablespoon prepared mustard
1	garlic clove, minced
3/4	cup dry bread crumbs
2	teaspoons dried basil
1	teaspoon paprika
1/2	teaspoon salt
1/4	teaspoon pepper
1	pound chicken tenderloins

In a shallow bowl, combine the egg substitute, mustard and garlic. In another shallow bowl, combine the bread crumbs, basil, paprika, salt and pepper. Dip chicken in egg mixture, then roll in crumbs.

Place on a baking sheet coated with cooking spray. Bake at 400° for 10-15 minutes or until golden brown and juices run clear. **Yield:** 4 servings.

Fresh vegetables and beans in a tasty tomato sauce make a hearty main dish. As an alternative, serve over pasta instead of in pastry shells.

TASTE OF HOME TEST KITCHEN

Bake Pastry Ahead: The puff pastry shells can be made a day in advance. Bake as directed; let cool. Place in an airtight container and store at room temperature.

30 vegetables in puff pastry

PREP/TOTAL TIME: 30 MIN.

1	package (10 ounces) frozen puff pastry shells
4	cups water
1	pound fresh baby carrots
1	teaspoon salt, *divided*
1	package (8 ounces) fresh sugar snap peas
1	medium leek (white portion only), sliced
1	teaspoon minced garlic
1	tablespoon butter
1	can (29 ounces) tomato puree
1	can (14-1/2 ounces) diced tomatoes, undrained
2	teaspoons sugar
2	teaspoons dried oregano
1/2	teaspoon pepper
1	package (16 ounces) frozen lima beans, thawed

Bake pastry shells according to package directions. Meanwhile, in a Dutch oven, bring the water to boil. Add carrots and 1/2 teaspoon salt. Reduce heat to medium; cook for 8-10 minutes or until tender. Add peas; cook for 1 minute. Drain and set aside.

In a large skillet, saute leek and garlic in butter until leek is crisp-tender. Add the tomato puree, tomatoes, sugar, oregano, pepper and remaining salt. Bring to a boil. Reduce heat. Add the lima beans and carrot mixture; cook for 5 minutes or until the vegetables are heated through. Remove tops from pastry shells; fill with vegetable mixture. **Yield:** 6 servings.

monday's dish

TUESDAY WEDNESDAY THURSDAY FRIDAY

GROCERIES/

- ☐ **4 boneless skinless chicken breast halves (4 ounces *each*)**
- ☐ **3/4 pound shaved deli ham**
- ☐ **1 pork tenderloin (1 pound)**
- ☐ **2 pounds ground beef**
- ☐ **8 plum tomatoes**
- ☐ **1 bunch fresh basil**
- ☐ **2 medium sweet potatoes**
- ☐ **1 medium red apple**
- ☐ **1 large onion**
- ☐ **4 green onions**
- ☐ **2 to 3 large tomatoes**
- ☐ **3 medium sweet red peppers**
- ☐ **3-1/2 cups instant *or* prepared refrigerated mashed potatoes**
- ☐ **Dried cranberries**
- ☐ **1 package (16 ounces) gemelli *or* spiral pasta**
- ☐ **1 envelope taco seasoning**
- ☐ **2 packages (10 ounces) frozen corn**
- ☐ **1 package (10 ounces) frozen peas**
- ☐ **1 package (8 ounces) round Brie cheese**
- ☐ **1 carton (8 ounces) sour cream**
- ☐ **3/4 cup shredded cheddar cheese**
- ☐ **2 cups (8 ounces) shredded cheddar cheese**
- ☐ **1 bag tortilla chips**
- ☐ **6 English muffins**

STAPLES/

- ▪ Beef bouillon ▪ Butter
- ▪ Cornstarch ▪ Dijon mustard
- ▪ Flour ▪ Garlic cloves
- ▪ Ketchup ▪ Mayonnaise ▪ Milk
- ▪ Oil (canola and olive)
- ▪ Pepper ▪ Salt ▪ Vinegar (balsamic and white)
- ▪ Worcestershire sauce

try a new dish every day...

This week's menu planner is packed with unexpected flavor that your family won't be able to resist! Basil gives ordinary grilled chicken an Italian twist...Brie cheese enlivens ham sandwiches...and taco seasoning turns mac 'n' cheese into a Southwest sensation. Meanwhile, shepherd's pie and a hearty pork dish offer old-fashioned comfort.

Relax after work with a cold drink while your savory chicken marinates, then toss it on the grill.

**LAURA LUNARDI
EXTON, PENNSYLVANIA**

A Lesson in Garlic: Minced garlic that you can buy, garlic that's been finely chopped by hand and garlic that's been put through a press can all be used interchangeably in recipes. Choose whichever is easiest and most convenient for you.

grilled basil chicken and tomatoes

PREP: 15 MIN. + MARINATING GRILL: 10 MIN.

8	plum tomatoes, *divided*
3/4	cup balsamic vinegar
1/4	cup tightly packed fresh basil leaves
2	tablespoons olive oil
1	garlic clove, minced
1/2	teaspoon salt
4	boneless skinless chicken breast halves (4 ounces *each*)

Cut four tomatoes into quarters and place in a food processor. Add the vinegar, basil, oil, garlic and salt; cover and process until blended.

Pour 1/2 cup dressing into a small bowl; cover and refrigerate until serving. Pour remaining dressing into a large resealable plastic bag; add chicken. Seal bag and turn to coat; refrigerate for up to 1 hour.

Coat grill rack with cooking spray before starting the grill. Drain and discard marinade. Grill chicken, covered, over medium heat for 4-6 minutes on each side or until a meat thermometer reads 170°.

Cut the remaining tomatoes in half; grill 2-3 minutes on each side or until tender. Serve with chicken and reserved dressing. **Yield:** 4 servings.

English muffins are a nice change for this classic French sandwich.

TASTE OF HOME TEST KITCHEN

ham 'n' brie sandwiches 20⟩

PREP/TOTAL TIME: 20 MIN.

1/3   cup mayonnaise
2   teaspoons Dijon mustard
1/2   teaspoon minced garlic
1/2   teaspoon white wine vinegar
1   package (8 ounces) round Brie cheese
6   English muffins, split
3/4   pound shaved deli ham
12   slices tomato

In a small bowl, combine the mayonnaise, mustard, garlic and vinegar until blended. Cut the Brie horizontally into three rounds; cut each round into eight wedges.

Place English muffins, cut side up, on a foil-lined 15-in. x 10-in. x 1-in. baking pan. Broil 3-4 in. from the heat for 2 minutes or until lightly toasted.

Spread muffins with mayonnaise mixture. Layer with ham, tomato and cheese wedges. Broil 3-4 in. from the heat for 5 minutes or until cheese is melted. **Yield:** 6 servings.

OUT OF ENGLISH MUFFINS?

If you don't have English muffins, these broiled sandwiches can be prepared with a variety of breads, including thick slices of French bread or kaiser rolls.

Sweet potatoes, sliced apple and moist pork tenderloin blend perfectly in this simple meal-in-one.

**MARY RELYEA
CANASTOTA
NEW YORK**

Crazy About Cranberries: Dried cranberries are a great way to boost the nutrition in foods throughout the day. Sprinkle them on cereal or your favorite salad. Mix some into breads and desserts. Or just eat them out of the bag for a healthy snack!

pork and sweet potatoes
PREP/TOTAL TIME: 30 MIN.

1	pork tenderloin (1 pound), cut into 12 slices
1/2	cup all-purpose flour
1/2	teaspoon salt
1/4	teaspoon pepper
1	tablespoon canola oil
1	can (14-1/2 ounces) chicken broth
2	medium sweet potatoes, peeled and cubed
1/2	cup dried cranberries
1	tablespoon Dijon mustard
1	medium red apple, sliced
4	green onions, chopped

Flatten pork to 1/4-in. thickness. In a large resealable plastic bag, combine the flour, salt and pepper; add pork, a few pieces at a time. Shake to coat.

In a large nonstick skillet coated with cooking spray, brown pork in oil in batches. Remove and keep warm. Add the broth, sweet potatoes and cranberries to the skillet. Bring to a boil. Reduce heat; cover and simmer for 4-6 minutes or until potatoes are almost tender. Stir in mustard.

Return pork to the pan; add apple and onions. Cover and simmer for 4-6 minutes or until meat juices run clear. **Yield:** 4 servings.

This is the best shepherd's pie I've ever tasted. It's very quick to make, and I usually have most— if not all—of the ingredients already on hand.

**TIRZAH SANDT
SAN DIEGO
CALIFORNIA**

Fast Fruit Salad: Cut up fresh fruit for a sweet side to serve with this meat and vegetable pie. You could also crack open a can of fruit cocktail, sliced pears or peaches or pineapple chunks.

skillet shepherd's pie 30

PREP/TOTAL TIME: 30 MIN.

1	pound ground beef
1	cup chopped onion
2	cups frozen corn, thawed
2	cups frozen peas, thawed
2	tablespoons ketchup
1	tablespoon Worcestershire sauce
2	teaspoons minced garlic
1	teaspoon beef bouillon granules
1/2	cup boiling water
1	tablespoon cornstarch
1/2	cup sour cream
3-1/2	cups mashed potatoes (prepared with milk and butter)
3/4	cup shredded cheddar cheese

In a large skillet, cook beef and onion over medium heat until meat is no longer pink; drain. Stir in the corn, peas, ketchup, Worcestershire sauce and garlic. Reduce heat; cover and simmer for 5 minutes.

Meanwhile, in a small bowl, dissolve bouillon in boiling water. Combine cornstarch and sour cream until smooth; stir into beef mixture until blended. Add bouillon mixture. Bring to a boil. Reduce heat, cook and stir until thickened.

Spread mashed potatoes over the top; sprinkle with cheese. Cover and cook until potatoes are heated through and cheese is melted. **Yield:** 6 servings.

Creamy and comforting, this casserole eases families into the week. Since most of the ingredients are mixed in one dish, cleanup is a breeze!

TASTE OF HOME TEST KITCHEN

Crazy for Corn: (tip)
A 10-ounce package of corn yields about 2 cups. Use one cup here and the other cup to make Mashed Potatoes with Corn and Cheese on page 175.

30 nacho mac 'n' cheese

PREP/TOTAL TIME: 25 MIN.

3	cups uncooked gemelli *or* spiral pasta
1	pound ground beef
2	cups chopped sweet red peppers
1/4	cup butter, cubed
1/4	cup all-purpose flour
1	envelope taco seasoning
1/4	teaspoon pepper
2-1/4	cups milk
2	cups (8 ounces) shredded cheddar cheese
1	cup frozen corn, thawed
1	cup coarsely crushed tortilla chips

Cook the gemelli according to package directions. Meanwhile, in a Dutch oven, cook beef and red peppers over medium heat until meat is no longer pink; drain.

Stir in the butter, flour, taco seasoning and pepper until blended. Gradually stir in milk. Bring to a boil; cook and stir for 2 minutes or until thickened. Remove from the heat. Stir in cheese and corn until cheese is melted.

Drain the gemelli; add to the beef mixture and stir to coat. Sprinkle with the tortilla chips. **Yield:** 6 servings.

friday's dish

MONDAY // TUESDAY WEDNESDAY THURSDAY

cut back on time...not flavor!

Surprise your family with quick-as-a-wink recipes that look like you spent hours preparing them. For a casual feel, serve the dishes family-style and let everyone help themselves. For something more special, plate the foods at the counter and present them to diners at the table. You'll find savory satisfaction with these five selections!

GROCERIES/

- ☐ 6 boneless skinless chicken breast halves (4 ounces *each*)
- ☐ 1-1/2 pounds halibut
- ☐ 1 pound boneless beef sirloin steak
- ☐ 1 large plus 1 small onion
- ☐ 8 green onions
- ☐ 1-1/2 cups finely chopped fresh pineapple
- ☐ 1 jalapeno pepper
- ☐ 1 head lettuce
- ☐ 1 pound whole mushrooms
- ☐ 1/2 pound sliced fresh mushrooms
- ☐ 2 large green peppers
- ☐ 1 medium sweet red pepper
- ☐ Fresh gingerroot
- ☐ 2 medium tomatoes
- ☐ Sherry
- ☐ 1 jar (2 ounces) diced pimientos
- ☐ 1 can (11 ounces) mandarin oranges
- ☐ 1 envelope taco seasoning
- ☐ 1 package (12 ounces) fettuccine
- ☐ 1 jar (7 ounces) sun-dried tomatoes (not packed in oil)
- ☐ 1 can (15-1/2 ounces) chili beans
- ☐ 1 can (8-3/4 ounces) whole kernel corn
- ☐ 1 package (10 ounces) frozen chopped spinach
- ☐ Orange juice concentrate
- ☐ 1 cup (8 ounces) sour cream
- ☐ 1 cup (4 ounces) shredded part-skim mozzarella cheese
- ☐ 1 cup (4 ounces) shredded Swiss cheese
- ☐ 8 corn tortillas (6 inches)

STAPLES/

- Baking powder ▪ Beef broth *or* beef bouillion ▪ Butter ▪ Chicken broth *or* chicken bouillon ▪ Cornmeal ▪ Cornstarch ▪ Dried basil and oregano ▪ Flour ▪ Garlic cloves ▪ Grated Parmesan ▪ Ground cumin ▪ Lime juice ▪ Milk ▪ Oil (canola and olive) ▪ Pepper ▪ Salt ▪ Soy sauce ▪ Sugar

Here is my very favorite chicken-and-spinach recipe. A creamy topping makes a pretty presentation.

**JULIE FITZGERALD
ST. LOUIS, MISSOURI**

Speedy Sauce: Prepare the spinach sauce the night before; cover and chill. Reheat before using.

30 > chicken with florentine sauce

PREP/TOTAL TIME: 30 MIN.

6	boneless skinless chicken breast halves (4 ounces *each*)
1/2	cup grated Parmesan cheese
1/2	teaspoon dried basil
1/2	teaspoon dried oregano
3	tablespoons butter, *divided*
2	green onions, chopped
1	teaspoon minced garlic
1	tablespoon all-purpose flour
1/4	teaspoon salt
1/2	cup milk
1	tablespoon sherry *or* chicken broth
1	package (10 ounces) frozen chopped spinach, thawed and squeezed dry
2	tablespoons diced pimientos
1/2	cup sour cream
1	cup (4 ounces) shredded part-skim mozzarella cheese

Flatten chicken to 1/2-in. thickness. In a large resealable plastic bag, combine the Parmesan cheese, basil and oregano. Add the chicken, a few pieces at a time, and shake to coat.

In a large skillet over medium heat, cook the chicken in 2 tablespoons of butter for 4-5 minutes on each side or until a meat thermometer reads 170°. Remove and keep warm.

In the same skillet, saute onions and garlic in remaining butter for 2-3 minutes or until tender. Gradually add flour and salt; stir in milk and sherry or broth until blended. Bring to a boil. Reduce heat; cook and stir for 1-2 minutes or until thickened. Stir in spinach and pimientos; heat through.

Remove from the heat. Stir in sour cream until blended. Spoon over chicken; sprinkle with mozzarella cheese. **Yield:** 6 servings.

My fun fish tacos bring a deliciously different twist to the Southwest standby! I combine halibut or cod with a fruity salsa and zesty seasoning.

MARIA BALDWIN
MESA, ARIZONA

(tip) **Purchase Pineapple:** If you don't want to buy, core and cut a whole pineapple, you can find cubed fresh pineapple in the produce or salad bar section of your grocery store.

citrus fish tacos

PREP: 15 MIN. + CHILLING BAKE: 15 MIN.

1-1/2	cups finely chopped fresh pineapple
1	can (11 ounces) mandarin oranges, drained and cut in half
1	envelope taco seasoning, *divided*
3	tablespoons thawed orange juice concentrate, *divided*
3	tablespoons lime juice, *divided*
1	jalapeno pepper, seeded and finely chopped
1-1/2	pounds halibut *or* cod, cut into 3/4-inch cubes
8	corn tortillas (6 inches), warmed
3	cups shredded lettuce

In a large bowl, combine fruit, 1 tablespoon taco seasoning, 1 tablespoon orange juice concentrate, 1 tablespoon lime juice and jalapeno pepper. Cover and refrigerate.

Place fish in an ungreased shallow 2-qt. baking dish. In a small bowl, combine the remaining orange juice concentrate, lime juice and taco seasoning. Pour over fish; toss gently to coat. Cover and bake at 375° for 12-16 minutes or until fish flakes easily with a fork.

Place a spoonful of fish mixture down the center of each tortilla. Top with lettuce and pineapple salsa; roll up. **Yield:** 4 servings.

EDITOR'S NOTE: When cutting hot peppers, disposable gloves are recommended. Avoid touching your face.

I can toss this dish together in 30 minutes on a busy weeknight. And it's elegant enough to serve as a vegetarian entree for guests.

**PHYLLIS SCHMALZ
KANSAS CITY
KANSAS**

Use Your Noodle:
Fettuccine, linguine, angel hair, spaghetti...there are oodles of noodles you can use for this dish!

fettuccine with mushrooms and tomatoes

PREP/TOTAL TIME: 30 MIN.

1	package (12 ounces) fettuccine
1	pound fresh mushrooms, halved
1	large onion, chopped
1	large green pepper, chopped
4	garlic cloves, minced
1	teaspoon olive oil
3	tablespoons all-purpose flour
3	cups 1% milk
1	teaspoon salt
1/4	teaspoon pepper
1/2	cup sun-dried tomatoes (not packed in oil), thinly sliced
1	cup (4 ounces) shredded Swiss cheese
1/4	cup grated Parmesan cheese

Cook fettuccine according to package directions. Meanwhile, in a large nonstick skillet, saute the mushrooms, onion, green pepper and garlic in oil for 4-6 minutes or until vegetables are tender.

In a small bowl, combine the flour, milk, salt and pepper until smooth; gradually stir into mushroom mixture. Add tomatoes. Bring to a boil; cook and stir for 2 minutes or until thickened. Stir in cheeses. Drain fettuccine; toss with sauce. **Yield:** 6 servings.

Loaded with hearty beans and corn, this tasty casserole is topped with a from-scratch corn bread.

DUANE AND CHRISTINE GEYER CORALVILLE, IOWA

Double the Recipe: Your family won't be able to eat just one serving of this Southwest casserole. So double the ingredients and bake it in a 13-in. x 9-in. baking dish for a bit longer.

southwest corn bread bake

PREP/TOTAL TIME: 30 MIN.

1	can (15-1/2 ounces) chili beans, undrained
1	can (8-3/4 ounces) whole kernel corn, drained
2	tablespoons chopped onion
1/2	teaspoon ground cumin
1/2	cup all-purpose flour
1/2	cup cornmeal
2	tablespoons sugar
1-1/4	teaspoons baking powder
1/4	teaspoon salt
1/2	cup plus 1 tablespoon milk
1-1/2	teaspoons canola oil

In a bowl, combine the chili beans, corn, onion and cumin. Transfer to an 8-in. square baking dish coated with cooking spray.

In another bowl, combine the dry ingredients. Combine milk and oil; stir into the dry ingredients just until moistened.

Drop by tablespoons over chili mixture; carefully spread over the top. Bake, uncovered, at 350° for 20-25 minutes or until golden brown. **Yield:** 4 servings.

A fast marinade flavors and tenderizes the sirloin steak in this colorful stir-fry.

**BILLIE MOSS
EL SOBRANTE
CALIFORNIA**

Give Gingerroot a Try:  Select gingerroot with a smooth skin. When stored in a plastic resealable bag, unpeeled gingerroot can be frozen for up to 1 year. When needed, simply peel and grate.

mushroom pepper steak

PREP: 15 MIN. + MARINATING   COOK: 15 MIN.

6	tablespoons soy sauce, *divided*
1/8	teaspoon pepper
1	pound boneless beef sirloin steak, cut into thin strips
1	tablespoon cornstarch
1/2	cup beef broth
1	garlic clove, minced
1/2	teaspoon minced fresh gingerroot
3	teaspoons canola oil, *divided*
1	cup julienned sweet red pepper
1	cup julienned green pepper
2	cups sliced fresh mushrooms
2	medium tomatoes, cut into wedges
6	green onions, cut into 1/2-inch pieces

Hot cooked rice, optional

In a large resealable plastic bag, combine 3 tablespoons soy sauce and pepper; add beef. Seal bag and turn to coat; refrigerate for 30-60 minutes. In a small bowl, combine the cornstarch, broth and remaining soy sauce until smooth; set aside.

Drain and discard marinade from beef. In a large nonstick skillet or wok, stir-fry the garlic and ginger in 2 teaspoons oil for 1 minute. Add the beef; stir-fry for 4-6 minutes or until no longer pink. Remove beef and keep warm.

Stir-fry the peppers in remaining oil for 1 minute. Add mushrooms; stir-fry 2 minutes longer or until peppers are crisp-tender. Stir broth mixture and add to vegetable mixture. Bring to a boil; cook and stir for 2 minutes or until thickened. Return beef to pan; add tomatoes and onions. Cook for 2 minutes or until heated through. Serve over rice if desired. **Yield:** 4 servings.

mini ham 'n' cheese frittatas, pg. 80

BREAKFAST

mini ham 'n' cheese frittatas

PREP: 15 MIN. **BAKE:** 25 MIN.

1/4	pound cubed fully cooked ham
1	cup (4 ounces) shredded cheddar cheese
6	eggs
4	egg whites
3	tablespoons minced chives
2	tablespoons milk
1/4	teaspoon salt
1/4	teaspoon pepper

Divide the ham evenly among eight muffin cups coated with cooking spray; top with the cheese. In a large bowl, beat the eggs and whites. Beat in the chives, milk, salt and pepper. Pour over the cheese, filling each muffin cup three-fourths full.

Bake at 375° for 22-25 minutes or until a knife inserted near the center comes out clean. Carefully run a knife around edges to loosen; remove from the pan. Serve warm. **Yield:** 8 frittatas.

I found this recipe a few years ago and tried to make it with a few changes. I often use fat-free ingredients to better suit my low-carb and low-fat diet.

SUSAN WATT
BASKING RIDGE
NEW JERSEY

Using Egg Substitute:
People who are watching their cholesterol often prefer to use egg substitute instead of whole eggs. Egg substitute can be used to replace whole eggs in many recipes with good results, especially in frittatas, omelets and quiches. One egg is equal to 1/4 cup egg substitute.

cherry-granola french toast sticks

PREP/TOTAL TIME: 20 MIN.

1/4	cup heavy whipping cream
3	tablespoons brown sugar
2	tablespoons butter
1	tablespoon dried cherries
1/4	teaspoon ground cinnamon
1/4	teaspoon vanilla extract
1	package (12.7 ounces) frozen French toast sticks
1	medium banana, sliced
1/4	cup granola without raisins

For syrup, in a small saucepan, combine the cream, brown sugar, butter, cherries and cinnamon. Bring to a boil over medium heat, stirring constantly. Cook and stir for 2 minutes. Remove from the heat; stir in the vanilla.

Prepare French toast sticks according to package directions. Serve with banana, granola and syrup. **Yield:** 4 servings.

The warm aroma of cinnamon and brown sugar helps wake my family. Convenient toast sticks topped with granola, banana and syrup carry them through busy days.

TERRI MCKITRICK
DELAFIELD, WISCONSIN

old-fashioned blueberry muffins

PREP/TOTAL TIME: 30 MIN.

1	cup all-purpose flour
1/3	cup sugar
1	teaspoon baking powder
1/4	teaspoon salt
1	egg
1/4	cup milk
2	tablespoons butter, melted
1/2	teaspoon vanilla extract
3/4	cup fresh *or* frozen blueberries

In a small bowl, combine the flour, sugar, baking powder and salt. In another bowl, whisk the egg, milk, butter and vanilla; stir into dry ingredients just until moistened. Fold in blueberries.

Fill greased or paper-lined muffin cups three-fourths full. Bake at 400° for 18-22 minutes or until a toothpick comes out clean. Cool for 5 minutes before removing from pan to a wire rack. Serve warm. **Yield: 6 muffins.**

EDITOR'S NOTE: If using frozen blueberries, do not thaw before adding to batter.

At the end of the summer years ago, our family often gathered to pick wild blueberries. Mother canned them and saved them for special pie treats during the holidays. If there were any leftover, she made them into these delicious blueberry muffins.

JUNE MORRIS
WATER MILL LONG ISLAND
NEW YORK

simple shrimp scramble

PREP/TOTAL TIME: 30 MIN.

1	small onion, chopped
1/4	cup chopped green pepper
1	garlic clove, minced
3	tablespoons butter, *divided*
1	package (5 ounces) frozen cooked salad shrimp, thawed
8	eggs, lightly beaten
1/2	teaspoon salt
1/4	teaspoon pepper
1	cup (4 ounces) shredded cheddar *or* Colby-Monterey Jack cheese

In a large skillet, saute the onion, green pepper and garlic in 1 tablespoon butter until tender. Stir in the shrimp. Remove to a bowl and keep warm.

In the same skillet, melt remaining butter over medium heat. Add eggs; cook and stir until completely set. Stir in the shrimp mixture, salt and pepper. Sprinkle with cheese.

Remove from the heat. Cover and let stand for 3-5 minutes or until the cheese is melted. **Yield:** 4 servings.

My husband is a big fan of breakfast. When I was looking for something different to make, I came up with this recipe. He raved over it.

PATTY CLONINGER
ROCHESTER, WASHINGTON

Save Some Shrimp:
The next time you serve shrimp, chop and set aside one cup so you can make Simple Shrimp Scramble the next morning.

six-fruit salad

PREP/TOTAL TIME: 10 MIN.

2	cups fresh strawberries, quartered
1	cup cubed honeydew
1/2	cup fresh blueberries
1	large apple, chopped
1	large navel orange, peeled and chopped
1	large ripe banana, cut into 1/4-inch slices
1/2	cup orange juice

In a large bowl, combine the fruit. Drizzle with orange juice and stir gently. Serve immediately. **Yield:** 8 servings.

This refreshing medley of fruits and berries is a favorite treat for breakfast and brunch.

PAULA BAGLOLE
SUMMERSIDE, PRINCE EDWARD ISLAND

BREAKFAST

calico pepper frittata

PREP/TOTAL TIME: 30 MIN.

1	medium green pepper, chopped
1	medium sweet red pepper, chopped
1	jalapeno pepper, seeded and chopped
1	medium onion, chopped
1	garlic clove, minced
1	tablespoon olive oil
5	eggs
1-1/4	cups egg substitute
1	tablespoon grated Romano cheese
1/2	teaspoon salt
1/8	teaspoon pepper

In a large nonstick skillet, saute peppers, onion and garlic in oil until crisp-tender. In a large bowl, whisk eggs and egg substitute. Pour into the skillet. Sprinkle with cheese, salt and pepper.

As the eggs set, lift edges, letting uncooked portion flow underneath. Cook until eggs are completely set, about 8-10 minutes. Cut into wedges. **Yield:** 4 servings.

EDITOR'S NOTE: When cutting hot peppers, disposable gloves are recommended. Avoid touching your face.

My garden-fresh frittata has all-day appeal. I serve it for breakfast, brunch, lunch and even dinner. It's made in a skillet, so there's no need to heat up the oven.

**LORETTA KELCINSKI
KUNKLETOWN
PENNSYLVANIA**

blended fruit chiller

PREP: 10 MIN.

3	cups (24 ounces) plain yogurt
1	cup unsweetened pineapple juice, chilled
1	cup fresh *or* frozen unsweetened strawberries
1	medium ripe banana, sliced
1/2	cup fresh *or* canned unsweetened pineapple chunks
3	tablespoons honey
1	teaspoon vanilla extract

Place half of each ingredient in a blender; cover and process until smooth. Pour into six chilled glasses. Repeat with the remaining ingredients. Serve chiller immediately. **Yield:** 6 servings.

This smoothie is great any time of the day. I especially like to serve it when my kids are in a finicky mood. It's a fun, nutritious breakfast.

KIRSTEN GUNDERSON
OTTAWA, ONTARIO

 Frozen Fruit Fact: When strawberries are in season, wash and hull a quart or two. Place in a shallow pan and freeze. When frozen, transfer to a heavy-duty resealable plastic bag. The berries can be kept frozen for up to 1 year without sacrificing flavor.

BREAKFAST

cinnamon swirl rolls

PREP/TOTAL TIME: 30 MIN.

1/3	cup packed brown sugar
1/4	cup sugar
1	teaspoon ground cinnamon
1	tube (11 ounces) refrigerated breadsticks
3	tablespoons butter, melted
3/4	cup confectioners' sugar
4	teaspoons milk
1/4	teaspoon vanilla extract

In a shallow bowl, combine the brown sugar, sugar and cinnamon. Separate dough into 12 breadsticks; brush all sides with butter, then coat with sugar mixture.

On a greased baking sheet, form three breadsticks into a coil, overlapping ends slightly. Secure with a toothpick through the overlapped ends and at the end of the swirl. Repeat with remaining breadsticks. Pour remaining butter over rolls; sprinkle with remaining sugar mixture.

Bake at 375° for 15-17 minutes or until golden brown. Remove to a wire rack. Discard toothpicks. Combine the confectioners' sugar, milk and vanilla; drizzle over rolls. Serve warm. **Yield:** 4 servings.

EDITOR'S NOTE: This recipe was tested with Pillsbury refrigerated breadsticks.

When you don't have time to make from-scratch cinnamon rolls, rely on this recipe that begins with refrigerated breadsticks. Employ little hands to help shape these sweet treats.

**TASTE OF HOME
TEST KITCHEN**

Quick & Easy Glaze:
Instead of making a confectioners' sugar glaze, heat up 1/2 cup vanilla frosting in the microwave and drizzle it over the rolls. Use leftover frosting to coat Cherry Cheese Danish on page 101.

breakfast rice pudding

PREP: 15 MIN. BAKE: 25 MIN.

1-1/3	cups uncooked long grain *or* basmati rice
1	can (15-1/4 ounces) peach halves, drained
1	cup canned *or* frozen pitted tart cherries, drained
1	cup heavy whipping cream
1/2	cup packed brown sugar, *divided*
1/4	cup old-fashioned oats
1/4	cup flaked coconut
1/4	cup chopped pecans
1/4	cup butter, melted

Cook rice according to package directions. In a large bowl, combine the rice, peaches, cherries, cream and 1/4 cup brown sugar. Transfer to a greased 1-1/2-quart baking dish.

Combine the oats, coconut, pecans, butter and remaining brown sugar; sprinkle over rice. Bake, uncovered, at 375° for 25-30 minutes or until golden brown. **Yield:** 8 servings.

My husband makes this rice pudding quite often for breakfast. It's equally good with fresh blueberries instead of cherries.

SUE DRAHEIM
WATERFORD, WISCONSIN

BREAKFAST

buttermilk waffles
PREP/TOTAL TIME: 25 MIN.

1-3/4	cups all-purpose flour
1	teaspoon baking powder
1	teaspoon baking soda
1/2	teaspoon salt
2	eggs
2	cups buttermilk
1/3	cup canola oil

Strawberry pancake syrup and whipped cream, optional

In a large bowl, combine the flour, baking powder, baking soda and salt. In another bowl, beat the eggs; add buttermilk and oil. Stir into dry ingredients just until combined.

Bake in a preheated waffle iron according to the manufacturer's directions until golden brown. Serve with syrup and whipped cream if desired. **Yield:** 16 waffles (4 inches).

You won't get any complaints from family or friends when you stack up these golden waffles for breakfast! My clan regularly requests this morning mainstay.

KIM BRANGES
GRAND CANYON, ARIZONA

Out of Buttermilk?
There are a number of substitutes for buttermilk. For each cup of buttermilk, you can use 1 tablespoon of white vinegar or lemon juice plus enough milk to measure 1 cup. Stir, then let stand for 5 minutes. You can also use 1 cup of plain yogurt or 1-3/4 teaspoons cream of tartar plus 1 cup milk.

mixed berry french toast bake

PREP: 20 MIN. + CHILLING BAKE: 45 MIN.

1	loaf (1 pound) French bread, cubed
6	egg whites
3	eggs
1-3/4	cups milk
1	teaspoon sugar
1	teaspoon ground cinnamon
1	teaspoon vanilla extract
1/4	teaspoon salt
1	package (12 ounces) frozen unsweetened mixed berries
2	tablespoons cold butter
1/3	cup packed brown sugar

Place bread cubes in a 13-in. x 9-in. baking dish coated with cooking spray. In a large bowl, combine the egg whites, eggs, milk, sugar, cinnamon, vanilla and salt; pour over bread. Cover and refrigerate for 8 hours or overnight.

Thirty minutes before baking, remove the berries from the freezer and set aside, and remove the baking dish from the refrigerator. Bake, covered, at 350° for 30 minutes.

In a small bowl, cut butter into brown sugar until crumbly. Sprinkle berries and brown sugar mixture over French toast. Bake, uncovered, for 15-20 minutes or until a knife inserted near the center comes out clean. **Yield:** 8 servings.

I love this recipe! Perfect for fuss-free holiday breakfasts or company, it's scrumptious and so easy to put together the night before.

AMY BERRY
POLAND, MAINE

cherry yogurt smoothies 10)

PREP/TOTAL TIME: 5 MIN.

1	cup cranberry juice
1	cup (8 ounces) cherry yogurt
1/2	cup cherry pie filling
1	medium ripe banana, cut into chunks
1	to 1-1/2 cups ice cubes

In a blender, combine all of the ingredients; cover and process until blended. Pour into chilled glasses; serve immediately. **Yield:** 4 servings.

I add some canned pie filling to create a special smoothie that's a favorite of mine. I think the cherries and banana are an awesome combination.

KATIE SLOAN
CHARLOTTE, NORTH CAROLINA

BREAKFAST

camper's breakfast hash

PREP/TOTAL TIME: 25 MIN.

1/4	cup butter, cubed
2	packages (20 ounces *each*) refrigerated shredded hash brown potatoes
1	package (7 ounces) brown-and-serve sausage links, cut into 1/2-inch pieces
1/4	cup chopped onion
1/4	cup chopped green pepper
12	eggs, lightly beaten

Salt and pepper to taste

1	cup (4 ounces) shredded cheddar cheese

In a large skillet, melt butter. Add the potatoes, sausage, onion and green pepper. Cook, uncovered, over medium heat for 10-15 minutes or until potatoes are lightly browned, turning once.

Push potato mixture to the sides of pan. Pour eggs into center of pan. Cook and stir over medium heat until eggs are completely set. Season with salt and pepper. Reduce heat; stir eggs into potato mixture. Top with cheese; cover and cook for 1-2 minutes or until cheese is melted. **Yield:** 8 servings.

When we go camping with family and friends, I'm always asked to make this hearty breakfast. It's a favorite at home, too.

LINDA KRIVANEK
OAK CREEK, WISCONSIN

pumpkin pancakes

PREP/TOTAL TIME: 20 MIN.

1-1/2	cups all-purpose flour
1/2	cup whole wheat flour
2	tablespoons brown sugar
2	teaspoons baking powder
1	teaspoon ground cinnamon
1/2	teaspoon salt
1/2	teaspoon ground ginger
1/2	teaspoon ground nutmeg
1-1/2	cups milk
1/2	cup canned pumpkin
1	egg white, lightly beaten
2	tablespoons canola oil

In a large bowl, combine the first eight ingredients. In a small bowl, combine the milk, pumpkin, egg white and oil; stir into dry ingredients just until moistened.

Pour batter by 1/4 cupfuls onto a hot griddle coated with cooking spray; turn when bubbles form on top. Cook until second side is golden brown. **Yield:** 6 servings.

I created these pumpkin-flavored pancakes with two kinds of flour and a blend of spices for a delightful taste. Serve them for brunch or for a fun meat-free dinner.

VICKI FLODEN
STORY CITY, IOWA

 Using Leftover Pumpkin: These pancakes call for 1/2 cup canned pumpkin. (A 15-ounce can equals 2 cups.) Use leftover pureed pumpkin to add flavor and nutrition to your favorite chili. Or add several heaping tablespoons to a package of instant vanilla pudding mix, reducing the amount of milk called for in the package directions by about 2-3 tablespoons.

pepperoni frittata

PREP/TOTAL TIME: 25 MIN.

1-1/4	cups chopped onions
2	to 3 tablespoons canola oil
1	cup sliced zucchini
1/2	cup small cauliflowerets
5	eggs, beaten
26	slices pepperoni
1/3	cup grated Parmesan cheese

In a 10-in. ovenproof skillet, saute the onions in oil until tender. Add the zucchini, cauliflower and eggs. Cover and cook over medium heat for 10-15 minutes or until eggs are nearly set.

Arrange the pepperoni over the eggs. Broil 6 in. from the heat for 2 minutes. Sprinkle with the Parmesan cheese; broil 1-2 minutes longer or until the eggs are completely set and the top is lightly browned. Cut into wedges. **Yield:** 6 servings.

We enjoy this fresh-tasting frittata with fresh fruit and toast. It even makes a good weeknight supper.

NANCY DALY
DOUGLAS, WYOMING

cranberry almond coffee cake

PREP: 20 MIN. BAKE: 45 MIN. + COOLING

1/2	cup almond paste
6	tablespoons butter, softened
1/2	cup plus 2 tablespoons sugar, *divided*
3	eggs
1-1/3	cups all-purpose flour, *divided*
1	teaspoon baking powder
1	teaspoon almond extract
1/2	teaspoon vanilla extract
2-1/4	cups fresh *or* frozen cranberries

In a small bowl, cream almond paste, butter and 1/2 cup sugar until fluffy. Add two eggs, beating well after each addition. Combine 1 cup flour and baking powder; add to creamed mixture. Beat in the remaining egg and flour. Stir in the extracts. Gently fold in cranberries.

Spread evenly into a greased 8-in. square baking dish; sprinkle with remaining sugar. Bake at 325° for 45-55 minutes or until a toothpick inserted near the center comes out clean. Cool on a wire rack. **Yield:** 9 servings.

Cranberries add a delightful tartness to this coffee cake that is a Christmas morning tradition for my family.

ANNE KEENAN
NEVADA CITY, CALIFORNIA

Homemade Almond Paste: Place 1-1/2 cups blanched almonds in a food processor; cover and process until smooth. Add 1-1/2 cups confectioners' sugar, 1 egg white, 1-1/2 teaspoons almond extract and 1/4 teaspoon salt; cover and process until smooth. Divide almond paste into 1/2-cup portions; place in airtight containers. Refrigerate for up to 1 month or freeze for up to 3 months.

crepes with berries

PREP: 15 MIN. + CHILLING COOK: 20 MIN.

2	tablespoons sugar
4	cups blueberries, blackberries *and/or* raspberries
1	cup milk
1	egg
3	egg whites
1/2	teaspoon almond extract
1/2	teaspoon vanilla extract
2/3	cup all-purpose flour
1/4	cup cornmeal
16	teaspoons apricot preserves
1	carton (8 ounces) vanilla yogurt

Sprinkle sugar over berries; gently toss to mix. Cover and refrigerate. In a blender, combine the milk, egg, egg whites and extracts; cover and process until blended. Add the flour and cornmeal; cover and process until blended. Cover and refrigerate for 1 hour.

Coat a 7-in. skillet with cooking spray. Heat skillet over medium heat. Pour about 2 tablespoons batter into the center of skillet. Lift and tilt pan to evenly coat bottom. Cook until top appears dry; turn and cook 15-20 seconds longer. Remove to a plate; keep warm. Repeat with remaining batter, coating with additional cooking spray as needed.

Spread each crepe with 1 teaspoon apricot preserves. Fold each crepe into quarters; place two crepes on an individual plate. Top with 2 tablespoons yogurt and 1/2 cup berry mixture. Serve immediately. **Yield:** 8 servings.

I like to greet the day in a luscious way—with homemade crepes served with berries and yogurt. The batter whips up easily in the blender.

LEICA MERRIAM
PROVIDENCE, UTAH

meatless sausage egg bake

PREP: 25 MIN. BAKE: 35 MIN. + STANDING

1	small onion, chopped
1	small green pepper, chopped
1	small sweet red pepper, chopped
2	teaspoons canola oil
12	egg whites
6	eggs
1	cup milk
1	package (16 ounces) frozen shredded hash brown potatoes, thawed
1	package (8 ounces) frozen vegetarian breakfast sausage patties, thawed and crumbled
1	cup (4 ounces) shredded cheddar cheese
1	teaspoon salt
1/2	teaspoon pepper

In a small nonstick skillet, saute onion and peppers in oil until tender. In a large bowl, beat the egg whites, eggs and milk. Stir in hash browns, crumbled sausage, cheese, salt, pepper and onion mixture.

Transfer to a 13-in. x 9-in. baking dish coated with cooking spray. Bake, uncovered, at 350° for 35-45 minutes or until a knife inserted near center comes out clean. Let stand 10 minutes before cutting. **Yield:** 8 servings.

This eye-opener is sure to please every palate at your breakfast table. Crumbled vegetarian patties make the potato casserole a hearty option that doesn't pack on the pounds.

**TASTE OF HOME
TEST KITCHEN**

Switch the Sausage: Regular pork breakfast sausage patties can be substituted for the meatless variety.

BREAKFAST

poppy seed muffins
PREP/TOTAL TIME: 30 MIN.

3/4 cup biscuit/baking mix
1/4 cup sugar
1-1/2 teaspoons poppy seeds
1 egg
1/3 cup sour cream
1/2 teaspoon vanilla extract

In a bowl, combine the biscuit mix, sugar and poppy seeds. In another bowl, whisk the egg, sour cream and vanilla; stir into dry ingredients just until moistened. Fill greased or paper-lined muffin cups two-thirds full.

Bake at 400° for 15-20 minutes or until a toothpick comes out clean. Cool for 5 minutes before removing from pan to a wire rack. Serve warm. **Yield:** 6 muffins.

My daughter fell in love with these tender, golden muffins when my sister made them for her. Sour cream adds a mild tang.

NANCY REGISTER
RALEIGH, NORTH CAROLINA

No-Stick Muffin Liners:
Spray paper liners with nonstick cooking spray before adding the muffin batter. The liner peels off very nicely, leaving no crumbs behind!

cran-strawberry cooler

PREP/TOTAL TIME: 15 MIN.

- 1-1/3   cups cranberry juice
- 2/3   cup white grape juice
- 9   to 10 fresh strawberries, *divided*
- 4   ice cubes
- 1/2   to 1 teaspoon sugar, optional

In a blender, combine the cranberry and grape juices, six strawberries, ice and sugar if desired. Cover and process until smooth. Serve in chilled glasses. Garnish with remaining strawberries. **Yield:** 3-4 servings.

This frothy refresher blends strawberries with cranberry juice, white grape juice and ice. The drink hits the spot whenever you serve it.

CLARA COULSTON
WASHINGTON COURT HOUSE, OHIO

vanilla yogurt ambrosia

PREP: 15 MIN. + CHILLING

- 1   can (20 ounces) pineapple tidbits, drained
- 1   can (11 ounces) mandarin oranges, drained
- 1-1/2   cups green grapes
- 1   cup miniature marshmallows
- 1/2   cup flaked coconut
- 1   carton (6 ounces) vanilla yogurt
- 1/4   cup chopped pecans, toasted

In a serving bowl, combine the pineapple, oranges, grapes, marshmallows and coconut. Fold in the yogurt. Cover and refrigerate for at least 1 hour. Just before serving, stir in pecans. **Yield:** 6 servings.

I have served this simple fruit salad many times, and it's always one of the first dishes to go.

SHERRY HULSMAN
LOUISVILLE, KENTUCKY

cornmeal pancakes

PREP/TOTAL TIME: 30 MIN.

- 1-1/3   cups all-purpose flour
- 2/3   cup cornmeal
- 2   tablespoons sugar
- 4   teaspoons baking powder
- 1   teaspoon salt
- 2   eggs
- 1-1/3   cups milk
- 1/4   cup canola oil

Pancake syrup

In a large bowl, combine the flour, cornmeal, sugar, baking powder and salt. In another bowl, whisk the eggs, milk and oil; stir into dry ingredients just until moistened.

Pour batter by 1/4 cupfuls onto a lightly greased hot griddle. Turn when bubbles form on top; cook until the second side is golden brown. Serve with syrup. **Yield:** 4 servings.

I like to joke that these pancakes are so light, you have to hold them down! When we have a chance, we'll make them with freshly ground cornmeal bought at local festivals.

BETTY CLAYCOMB
ALVERTON, PENNSYLVANIA

special stuffed french toast

PREP: 20 MIN. COOK: 15 MIN.

1	cup plus 2 tablespoons sugar, *divided*
2	tablespoons cornstarch
3/4	cup water
4	cups pitted frozen tart cherries, thawed
1	package (8 ounces) cream cheese, softened
1	cup confectioners' sugar
12	slices Texas toast
1	egg
1	cup milk

For cherry sauce, combine 1 cup sugar and cornstarch in a small saucepan. Stir in the water until smooth. Add cherries. Bring to a boil; cook and stir for 1-2 minutes or until thickened. Remove from the heat and set aside.

In a small bowl, beat cream cheese and confectioners' sugar until smooth. Spread over six slices of bread; top with remaining bread. In a shallow bowl, whisk the egg, milk and remaining sugar. Dip both sides of bread into egg mixture.

In a large nonstick skillet coated with cooking spray, toast bread on both sides until golden brown. Serve with cherry sauce. **Yield:** 6 servings.

For a breakfast or brunch sensation, whip up this dish showcasing cherries. The golden-brown Texas toast is delectable with cream cheese tucked between thick slices. The sweet-tart cherry sauce makes a pretty and flavorful topping.

ROBIN PERRY
SENECA, PENNSYLVANIA

Do-Ahead Idea:
Avoid an early morning rush by making the cherry sauce the night before. Cover and chill. Reheat over low before serving with the French toast.

bacon 'n' egg burritos

PREP/TOTAL TIME: 25 MIN.

6	bacon strips, diced
1	cup frozen Southern-style hash brown potatoes
2	tablespoons chopped onion
6	eggs
1/4	cup sour cream
3/4	cup shredded cheddar cheese, *divided*
2	tablespoons taco sauce
1/2	to 1 teaspoon hot pepper sauce
4	flour tortillas (10 inches), warmed

Sour cream and chopped tomatoes, optional

In a large skillet, cook bacon over medium heat until crisp. Using a slotted spoon, remove to paper towels; drain, reserving 1 tablespoon drippings. Add the potatoes and onion to drippings; cook and stir over medium heat until potatoes are golden brown.

In a large bowl, whisk eggs and sour cream. Stir in 1/4 cup cheese, taco sauce and hot pepper sauce. Pour over potato mixture; add bacon. Cook and stir over medium heat until eggs are completely set.

Spoon about 3/4 cup down the center of each tortilla; sprinkle with remaining cheese. Fold bottom and sides of tortilla over filling. Serve immediately with sour cream and tomatoes if desired. **Yield:** 4 servings.

My husband and I discovered these delicious burritos when we drove truck as a team in the Southwestern U.S. Jason created this version that our guests enjoy as much as we do.

ROBYN LARABEE
LUCKNOW, ONTARIO

banana berry drink

PREP/TOTAL TIME: 10 MIN.

3/4	cup orange juice, chilled
1/3	cup pineapple juice, chilled
1	cup frozen blueberries
1/2	cup frozen sweetened sliced strawberries
1/2	cup plain yogurt
1	small ripe banana, sliced

Place half of each ingredient in a blender; cover and process until smooth. Pour into chilled glasses. Repeat with remaining ingredients. Serve immediately. **Yield:** 5 servings.

A cold refreshing beverage is a great substitute for breakfast when you're in a hurry.

ERIC KNOBEN
EDGEWOOD, WASHINGTON

30

almond-apple coffee cake

PREP/TOTAL TIME: 30 MIN.

1-1/2   cups thinly sliced peeled tart apples
3   tablespoons brown sugar
1   tablespoon lemon juice
3/4   teaspoon apple pie spice
2   tablespoons butter, softened
1/3   cup sugar
1   egg
1   teaspoon vanilla extract
1   cup all-purpose flour
1/2   teaspoon baking soda
1/8   teaspoon salt
1/2   cup buttermilk
1   tablespoon sliced almonds

GLAZE:
1/4   cup confectioners' sugar
1   teaspoon buttermilk
1/4   teaspoon vanilla extract

In a large saucepan, combine the apples, brown sugar, lemon juice and apple pie spice. Cook over medium-high heat for 5 minutes or until syrup is thickened and apples are tender, stirring occasionally.

In a small bowl, cream butter and sugar. Beat in egg and vanilla. Combine flour, baking soda and salt; add to creamed mixture alternately with buttermilk. Spoon batter into a greased 9-in. springform pan. Arrange apple mixture over top; sprinkle with almonds.

Bake at 350° for 20-25 minutes or until a toothpick inserted near the center comes out clean. Cool on wire rack. Remove sides of pan. Combine glaze ingredients; drizzle over top. **Yield:** 8 servings.

I make this moist and tangy coffee cake for small gatherings or to give to a friend in need of a little cheer.

CATHY CLEMONS
NARROWS, VIRGINIA

cherry cheese danish

PREP/TOTAL TIME: 30 MIN.

1	tube (8 ounces) refrigerated crescent rolls
4	tablespoons cream cheese, softened
1	cup cherry pie filling
1/2	cup vanilla frosting

Separate the crescent dough into four rectangles. Place on an ungreased baking sheet; seal perforations. Spread 1 tablespoon cream cheese onto each rectangle. Top each with 1/4 cup cherry pie filling.

Bake at 375° for 10-12 minutes or until edges are golden brown. Cool for 5 minutes.

Place frosting in a small microwave-safe bowl; heat on high for 15-20 seconds. Drizzle over warm pastries. Serve warm. Refrigerate leftovers. **Yield:** 4 servings.

Here is a quick Sunday breakfast I like to whip up before going to church. I created it when trying to duplicate a favorite Danish from the bakery where I worked.

MELANIE SCHROCK
MONTEREY, TENNESSEE

 Favorite Filling: If your family isn't fond of cherries, use a different pie filling, such as apple, blueberry or lemon.

BREAKFAST

asparagus eggs benedict

PREP/TOTAL TIME: 15 MIN.

12	fresh asparagus spears, trimmed and cut in half
1	envelope hollandaise sauce mix
6	eggs
3	English muffins, split and toasted
1/2	cup shredded Swiss cheese

Paprika

Place asparagus in a steamer basket. Place in a large saucepan over 1 in. of water; bring to a boil. Cover and steam for 3-4 minutes or until crisp-tender. Set aside.

Prepare hollandaise sauce according to package directions. Meanwhile, in a large skillet, bring 2-3 in. water to a boil. Reduce heat; simmer gently. Break cold eggs, one at a time, into a custard cup or saucer. Holding the dish close to the surface of the water, slip the eggs, one at a time, into the water.

Cook, uncovered, for 3-5 minutes or until the whites are completely set and the yolks begin to thicken. With a slotted spoon, lift each egg out of the water.

To assemble, place 4 pieces of asparagus on each muffin half; top with a poached egg, then sprinkle with cheese. Top each with about 3 tablespoons hollandaise sauce; garnish with paprika. Serve immediately. **Yield:** 6 servings.

Eggs Benedict is a favorite springtime Sunday brunch item at our house.

MARK MORGAN
WATERFORD, WISCONSIN

Poaching Pointers:
For perfect poached eggs, use the freshest eggs possible. Adding 2 tablespoons of vinegar and a dash of salt for each quart of water will help keep the eggs from spreading.

greatest granola

PREP: 15 MIN. BAKE: 25 MIN. + COOLING

2	cups old-fashioned oats
1	cup Grape-Nuts
1/2	cup sliced almonds
1/2	cup honey
1/3	cup canola oil
1/4	cup packed brown sugar
1-1/2	teaspoons vanilla extract
1/4	teaspoon ground cinnamon
1	cup crisp rice cereal
1/2	cup toasted wheat germ
1/2	cup chopped dried apricots
1/2	cup dried cranberries, chopped

Yogurt flavor of your choice, optional

In a large bowl, combine the oats, Grape-Nuts and almonds. Spread into a greased, foil-lined 15-in. x 10-in. x 1-in. baking pan. Coat mixture with cooking spray. Bake, uncovered, at 300° for 20 minutes, stirring once.

Meanwhile, in a small saucepan, combine the honey, oil and brown sugar. Cook and stir over low heat until heated through. Remove from the heat; stir in vanilla and cinnamon.

Stir cereal and wheat germ into oat mixture. Drizzle with honey mixture; stir to coat. Bake 5-10 minutes longer or until golden brown. Cool on a wire rack.

Break granola into pieces. Sprinkle with apricots and cranberries and mix well. Store in an airtight container. Serve with yogurt if desired. **Yield:** about 8 cups.

After clipping granola recipes for years, I chose my favorite ingredients from each one, added a few of my own and came up with this tasty version. My family thinks it's the greatest!

JONIE DAIGLE
GREENSBURG
PENNSYLVANIA

ham 'n' cheese squares

PREP: 15 MIN. BAKE: 20 MIN.

1-1/2	cups cubed fully cooked ham
1	carton (6 ounces) plain yogurt
1/4	cup crushed saltines (about 6)
1/4	cup shredded Swiss cheese
2	tablespoons butter, melted
2	teaspoons caraway seeds
6	eggs

In a large bowl, combine the first six ingredients. In a small bowl, beat eggs until thickened and lemon-colored; fold into ham mixture. Transfer to a greased 8-in. square baking dish.

Bake at 375° for 20-25 minutes or until a knife inserted near the center comes out clean. Let stand for 5 minutes before cutting. **Yield:** 9 servings.

So easy to prepare, this appetizing egg dish is loaded with ham, Swiss cheese and caraway flavor. It cuts nicely into squares, making it an ideal addition to a buffet.

SUE ROSS
CASA GRANDE, ARIZONA

cheesy sausage potatoes

PREP/TOTAL TIME: 25 MIN.

30

3	pounds potatoes, peeled and cut into 1/4-inch slices
1	pound bulk pork sausage
1	medium onion, chopped
1/4	cup butter, melted
2	cups (8 ounces) shredded cheddar cheese

Place potatoes in a large saucepan and cover with water. Bring to a boil. Reduce heat; simmer, uncovered, for 8-10 minutes or until tender. Meanwhile, crumble sausage into a large skillet; add onion. Cook over medium heat until meat is no longer pink; drain if necessary.

Drain potatoes; arrange in an ungreased 13-in. x 9-in. baking dish. Drizzle with butter. Add sausage mixture and stir gently. Sprinkle with cheese.

Bake, uncovered, at 350° for 5-7 minutes or until cheese is melted. **Yield:** 6-8 servings.

For a satisfying brunch, try these tender potato slices with lots of sausage and cheese. Everyone loves them, and the pan is always empty.

LINDA HILL
MARSEILLES, ILLINOIS

Peeling Potatoes: Peel and slice the potatoes in advance. Completely cover with water and refrigerate. The next morning, drain well and cook as directed.

BREAKFAST

breakfast loaf

PREP: 15 MIN. BAKE: 25 MIN.

6	eggs, lightly beaten
1/4	teaspoon salt
1/8	teaspoon pepper
1	tablespoon butter
1	round loaf (1 pound) French bread
6	ounces thinly sliced deli ham, *divided*
3/4	cup shredded Monterey Jack cheese, *divided*
3/4	cup shredded cheddar cheese, *divided*
1/2	medium sweet red pepper, thinly sliced
1	medium tomato, thinly sliced

In a small bowl, combine eggs, salt and pepper. Melt butter in a skillet; add eggs. Cook and stir until set; set aside. Cut off the top fourth of the bread. Carefully hollow out top and bottom, leaving a 1/2-in. shell. (Discard removed bread or save for another use.) Set top aside.

In bottom of bread, place a fourth of the ham. Layer with half of the Monterey Jack and cheddar cheeses, red pepper, scrambled eggs and tomato slices. Top with the remaining cheese and ham. Gently press the layers together. Replace bread top and wrap tightly in foil. Bake at 350° for 25-30 minutes or until heated through. Let stand for 10 minutes before cutting. **Yield:** 6 servings.

I love to make this hearty sandwich when we have company for the weekend. If you like, add sliced mushrooms and olives.

AMY MCCUAN
OAKLEY, CALIFORNIA

Add Herb Flavor: To give scrambled eggs great herb flavor, sprinkle in some finely chopped dill or chives.

omelet wedges with cheese sauce

PREP/TOTAL TIME: 30 MIN.

6	eggs, *separated*
1/2	teaspoon salt
1/4	cup cornstarch
Dash pepper	
1/3	cup water

SAUCE:

1	tablespoon butter
1	tablespoon cornstarch
1/4	teaspoon salt
Dash pepper	
1	cup milk
2	cups (8 ounces) shredded cheddar cheese

In a small bowl, beat egg whites and salt until stiff peaks form. In a large bowl, beat the cornstarch, egg yolks and pepper until lemon-colored. Add water; mix well. Fold in the egg whites.

Pour into two greased 9-in. pie plates. Bake at 350° for 15 minutes or until a knife inserted near the center comes out clean.

Meanwhile, in a small saucepan, melt butter. Stir in the cornstarch, salt and pepper until smooth. Gradually add milk. Bring to a boil; cook and stir for 2 minutes or until thickened. Reduce heat; stir in the cheese until melted.

To serve, cut each omelet into six wedges. Stack two wedges on each serving plate with cheese sauce drizzled between and on top. **Yield:** 6 servings.

Our kids wake up early when this fluffy, layered omelet is on the menu. A savory cheese sauce tastefully tops each piece.

AMY TRANSUE
CATASAUQUA
PENNSYLVANIA

tex-mex cheese strata

PREP: 15 MIN. + CHILLING BAKE: 40 MIN. + STANDING

4	cups coarsely crushed nacho tortilla chips
2	cups (8 ounces) shredded Monterey Jack cheese
1	small onion, finely chopped
1	tablespoon butter
6	eggs
2-1/2	cups milk
1	can (4 ounces) chopped green chilies, undrained
3	tablespoons ketchup
1/4	teaspoon hot pepper sauce

Arrange tortilla chips in a greased 13-in. x 9-in. baking dish; sprinkle with the cheese and set aside. In a skillet, saute the onion in butter until tender. In a bowl, whisk the eggs, milk, onion, chilies, ketchup and hot pepper sauce; pour over cheese. Cover and refrigerate overnight.

Remove from the refrigerator 30 minutes before baking. Bake, uncovered, at 350° for 40-45 minutes or until a thermometer reads 160° and a knife inserted near the center comes out clean. Let stand for 5 minutes before cutting. **Yield:** 6-8 servings.

Tortilla chips add a little fun to this South-of-the-border brunch dish. For spicier flavor, substitute Pepper Jack for the Monterey Jack cheese.

VICKIE LOWREY
FALLON, NEVADA

christmas cocoa

PREP/TOTAL TIME: 15 MIN.

4	cups milk
2/3	cup instant chocolate drink mix
5	chocolate mint candy canes, crushed
1-1/2	cups heavy whipping cream
1/4	cup confectioners' sugar
1/2	teaspoon vanilla extract

In a large saucepan, combine the milk and drink mix. Cook and stir over medium heat until heated through. Remove from the heat. Set aside 1 tablespoon crushed candy canes for garnish. Stir remaining candy canes into cocoa; keep warm.

In a small bowl, beat cream until it begins to thicken. Add confectioners' sugar and vanilla; beat until stiff peaks form. Ladle the cocoa into mugs. Top with the whipped cream; sprinkle with the reserved crushed candy canes. **Yield:** 4 servings.

A sprinkling of crushed candy cane lends a festive touch to this creamy hot cocoa...or place a chocolate mint candy cane in each mug as a stirrer.

LORI DANIELS
BEVERLY, WEST VIRGINIA

 Whipping Cream: For best results, start with cold whipping cream. Choose a deep metal bowl, as the cream will double in volume. Place the bowl and beaters in the freezer for at least 15 minutes before using. Beat quickly until stiff peaks form, scraping the bowl occasionally.

breakfast sausage patties

PREP/TOTAL TIME: 20 MIN.

1	pound ground turkey
3/4	teaspoon salt
1/2	teaspoon rubbed sage
1/2	teaspoon dried thyme
1/2	teaspoon ground nutmeg
1/8	teaspoon cayenne pepper
2	teaspoons canola oil

In a large bowl, combine the turkey, salt, sage, thyme, nutmeg and cayenne. Shape into eight patties.

In a large skillet, cook patties in oil over medium heat for 5 minutes on each side or until juices run clear. Drain on paper towels. **Yield:** 4 servings.

These breakfast patties are the perfect accompaniment to any egg entree. Cayenne pepper gives the sausage just the right amount of zip.

CAROLYN SYKORA
BLOOMER, WISCONSIN

BREAKFAST

rhubarb cream muffins

PREP: 20 MIN. BAKE: 15 MIN.

1/4	cup butter, softened
3/4	cup packed brown sugar
1	egg
1	cup all-purpose flour
1/2	teaspoon baking powder
1/2	teaspoon baking soda
1/4	teaspoon salt
1/2	cup sour cream
3/4	cup diced fresh *or* frozen rhubarb
1/4	cup chopped walnuts

TOPPING:

1/4	cup sugar
1/2	teaspoon ground cinnamon
1	tablespoon cold butter

In a large bowl, cream butter and brown sugar until light and fluffy. Add egg; mix well. Combine the flour, baking powder, baking soda and salt; add to creamed mixture alternately with sour cream. Fold in rhubarb and walnuts.

Fill paper-lined muffin cups three-fourths full. For the topping, combine sugar and cinnamon in a bowl; cut in the butter until crumbly. Sprinkle over batter.

Bake at 375° for 15-20 minutes or until a toothpick comes out clean. Cool for 5 minutes before removing from pan to a wire rack. Serve warm. **Yield:** 8 muffins.

EDITOR'S NOTE: If using frozen rhubarb, measure rhubarb while still frozen, then thaw completely. Drain in a colander, but do not press liquid out.

My friend Barbara gave me this recipe, and it's easy to double. The tender, golden muffins have a mild rhubarb flavor and a yummy cinnamon topping.

**MARGARET GUEST
TRENTON, ONTARIO**

hearty brunch pockets

PREP/TOTAL TIME: 25 MIN.

6	brown-and-serve sausage links, sliced
6	ready-to-serve fully cooked bacon strips, diced
6	eggs
2	tablespoons milk
1	teaspoon salt
1/4	teaspoon pepper
1	cup (4 ounces) shredded Colby-Monterey Jack cheese
3	pita breads (6 inches), halved

In a nonstick skillet, cook sausage for 2 minutes. Add bacon; cook 4 minutes longer or until sausage is heated through and bacon is crisp. Remove and keep warm.

In a small bowl, whisk the eggs, milk, salt and pepper. Pour into the skillet; cook and stir over medium heat until eggs are almost set. Add sausage mixture and cheese. Cook and stir for 2 minutes or until eggs are completely set and cheese is melted. Spoon into pita halves. **Yield:** 6 servings.

I made this recipe up one night when I was looking for a quick and tasty meal for myself and my kids. It was an instant hit! It makes a great entree any time of the day.

MEREDITH BEYL
STILLWATER, OKLAHOMA

tip

Zesty Side: Add a little spice to your morning meal by serving salsa alongside these egg and sausage pockets.

BREAKFAST

farmer's breakfast

PREP/TOTAL TIME: 30 MIN.

3	cups finely chopped peeled potatoes (about 3 medium)
1/4	cup chopped green pepper
3	tablespoons butter
9	eggs
3	tablespoons milk
1/4	teaspoon pepper
1-1/2	cups cubed fully cooked ham
1	jar (4-1/2 ounces) sliced mushrooms, drained
1/4	cup shredded cheddar cheese

In a 2-qt. microwave-safe dish, combine the potatoes, green pepper and butter. Cover and microwave on high for 7-8 minutes or until vegetables are tender, stirring once.

In a large bowl, beat the eggs, milk and pepper; stir in ham and mushrooms. Stir into potato mixture. Cover and microwave at 70% power for 8-10 minutes or until eggs are almost set, stirring every 2 minutes.

Sprinkle with the cheese. Cook, uncovered, on high for 1-2 minutes or until the cheese is melted and the eggs are completely set. **Yield:** 6 servings.

EDITOR'S NOTE: This recipe was tested in a 1,100-watt microwave.

I found this recipe in the newspaper several years ago and loved it. Whenever I serve it to overnight guests, I'm asked for the recipe.

LYNN AMES
IDAHO FALLS, IDAHO

hot colby ham sandwiches, pg. 130

SOUPS & SANDWICHES

SOUPS & SANDWICHES

chicken wraps

PREP/TOTAL TIME: 25 MIN.

16   frozen breaded chicken tenders
1/2   cup ranch salad dressing
4   sun-dried tomato tortillas (10 inches), room temperature
3   cups shredded lettuce
1   can (2-1/4 ounces) sliced ripe olives, drained
4   slices pepper Jack cheese
Hot pepper sauce, optional

Bake chicken according to package directions. Meanwhile, spread 2 tablespoons salad dressing over each tortilla. Sprinkle lettuce and olives down the center of each tortilla. Top with cheese and chicken; drizzle with hot pepper sauce if desired. Roll up; secure with toothpicks. **Yield:** 4 servings.

This wrap makes a lunch that's quick, easy and delicious. Just as good served cold, you can bake your chicken the night before and assemble your sandwich the next day.

KARIMA ALARHABI
GARYSBURG
NORTH CAROLINA

Try Other Tortillas:
Make these roll-ups with any flavor of tortillas or wraps you prefer. Options include spinach, tomato basil, garlic herb, chipotle and whole wheat.

wild rice chicken soup

PREP/TOTAL TIME: 30 MIN.

1/4	cup *each* chopped carrot, celery, green pepper and onion
1/4	cup chopped peeled parsnip
2	teaspoons canola oil
2	cans (14-1/2 ounces *each*) chicken broth
3/4	pound bone-in chicken thighs, skin removed
1/2	teaspoon dried savory
1	garlic clove, minced
1/8	teaspoon salt
1/8	teaspoon pepper
1	cup cooked long grain and wild rice

In a large saucepan, saute the carrot, celery, green pepper, onion and parsnip in oil for 3 minutes or until crisp-tender. Add the broth, chicken, savory, garlic, salt and pepper. Bring to a boil. Reduce heat; cover and simmer for 15 minutes or until chicken juices run clear.

Remove chicken from broth. When cool enough to handle, remove meat from bones and cut into bite-size pieces. Discard bones. Add chicken and rice to soup; heat through. **Yield:** 5 cups.

This hearty soup is chock-full of tender thigh meat and veggies and is pleasantly seasoned with savory and garlic.

TASTE OF HOME
TEST KITCHEN

SOUPS & SANDWICHES

 kids' favorite chili

PREP/TOTAL TIME: 25 MIN.

1	pound ground turkey
1/2	cup chopped onion
1	can (15-3/4 ounces) pork and beans
1	can (14-1/2 ounces) diced tomatoes, undrained
1	can (10-3/4 ounces) condensed tomato soup, undiluted
1	tablespoon brown sugar
1	tablespoon chili powder

In a large saucepan, cook turkey and onion over medium heat until meat is no longer pink; drain. Stir in the remaining ingredients. Bring to a boil. Reduce heat; cover and simmer for 15-20 minutes or until heated through. **Yield:** 4 servings.

This sweet and easy chili is sure to warm the whole family up on those chilly fall nights.

TERRI KEENEY
GREELEY, COLORADO

Easy Quesadillas: Cheese quesadillas pair well with chili. Place four 8-in. tortillas on a greased baking sheet. Combine 1-1/2 cups shredded Mexican cheese blend with 1/2 cup salsa; spread over half of each tortilla. Fold over. Broil for 3 minutes on each side until golden brown. Cut into wedges.

pesto roast beef sub

PREP/TOTAL TIME: 30 MIN.

1	cup loosely packed basil leaves
2	tablespoons grated Parmesan cheese
1	tablespoon chopped dill pickle
1	tablespoon white wine vinegar
2	teaspoons Dijon mustard
1	garlic clove, peeled
1/4	cup olive oil
1	loaf (1 pound) unsliced French bread
1/2	pound thinly sliced deli roast beef
4	slices provolone cheese
1	medium tomato, thinly sliced
1-1/2	cups fresh baby spinach

For pesto, in a food processor, combine the basil, Parmesan cheese, pickle, vinegar, mustard and garlic; cover and process until chopped. While processing, gradually add oil in a steady stream; process until blended.

Cut the loaf of bread in half horizontally. Hollow out bottom half, leaving a 3/4-in. shell (discard removed bread or save for another use). Spread two-thirds of the pesto inside shell; layer with beef, cheese, tomato and spinach. Spread remaining pesto over cut side of bread top; place over sandwich. Cut into slices to serve. **Yield:** 6-8 servings.

In this scrumptious sandwich, I dress up deli roast beef with a fast-to-fix pesto.

PATRICIA KILE
GREENTOWN, PENNSYLVANIA

sesame hot dogs

PREP/TOTAL TIME: 30 MIN.

8	hot dogs
1/4	cup sharp American cheese spread
1	tube (16.3 ounces) large refrigerated buttermilk biscuits
2	tablespoons butter, melted
1/4	cup sesame seeds

Make a lengthwise slit three-quarters of the way through each hot dog to within 1/2 in. of each end. Spread cheese into pockets. Roll each biscuit into a 5-in. circle; wrap one around each hot dog. Brush with butter and roll in sesame seeds.

Place on a lightly greased baking sheet. Bake at 425° for 11-13 minutes or until golden brown. **Yield:** 8 servings.

Kids of all ages love these cute, cheese-stuffed hot dogs wrapped in crusty, sesame-seed biscuits. I serve them with bowls of chili, mustard, ketchup...even bean dip or salsa for dipping.

SUE MACKEY
GALESBURG, ILLINOIS

SOUPS & SANDWICHES

 hot turkey bunwiches

PREP/TOTAL TIME: 30 MIN.

1-1/2	cups chopped cooked turkey
2	hard-cooked eggs, chopped
1/3	cup chopped onion
1/2	cup chopped celery
1/2	cup cubed sharp cheddar cheese
1/2	cup mayonnaise
1/8	teaspoon salt
1/8	teaspoon pepper
4	teaspoons butter, softened
4	sandwich buns, split

In a large bowl, combine the first eight ingredients. Spread butter over cut sides of each bun. Spread about 2/3 cup turkey salad over each bun bottom; replace tops. Wrap individually in foil.

Place buns on a baking sheet. Bake at 375° for 15-20 minutes or until the cheese is melted. **Yield:** 4 servings.

Put leftover turkey and hard-boiled eggs to tasty use in warm and buttery sandwiches. Everyone in our family looks forward to these bunwiches.

PATTY COSTANTINO
CANONSBURG
PENNSYLVANIA

shrimp soup with sherry

PREP/TOTAL TIME: 30 MIN.

1/4	cup sliced green onions
3	tablespoons butter
1/4	cup all-purpose flour
1	teaspoon ground mustard
1	pinch cayenne pepper
2	cups half-and-half cream
1	cup chicken broth
2	tablespoons minced fresh parsley
1/8	teaspoon dried thyme
1/8	teaspoon hot pepper sauce
1/8	teaspoon Worcestershire sauce
1-1/4	cups cooked small shrimp, peeled and deveined
1/4	cup dry sherry *or* additional chicken broth

Salt and pepper to taste

In a large saucepan, saute onions in butter until tender. Stir in the flour, mustard and cayenne until blended; gradually add cream and broth. Bring to a boil; cook and stir for 2 minutes or until thickened.

Stir in the parsley, thyme, hot pepper sauce and Worcestershire sauce. Cover and cook over low heat for 10 minutes, stirring occasionally. Add shrimp and sherry or additional broth; heat through. Season with salt and pepper. **Yield:** 4 servings.

This rich soup makes a great first course when small servings are just right. It's a festive addition to any menu.

MARILYN GRANER
METAIRIE, LOUISIANA

Don't Have Half-and-Half?
If you forgot to pick up half-and-half cream while shopping, you may substitute 4-1/2 teaspoons melted butter plus enough whole milk to equal 1 cup. One cup of evaporated milk may also be used for each cup of half-and-half.

SOUPS & SANDWICHES

 ## meat and potato soup

PREP/TOTAL TIME: 30 MIN.

4 cups water
3 cups cubed cooked beef chuck roast
4 medium red potatoes, cubed
4 ounces sliced fresh mushrooms
1/2 cup chopped onion
1/4 cup ketchup
2 teaspoons beef bouillon granules
2 teaspoons cider vinegar
1 teaspoon brown sugar
1 teaspoon Worcestershire sauce
1/8 teaspoon ground mustard
1 cup coarsely chopped fresh spinach

In a Dutch oven, combine the first 11 ingredients. Bring to a boil. Reduce heat; cover and simmer for 14-18 minutes or until the potatoes are tender. Stir in the spinach; cook 1-2 minutes longer or until tender. **Yield:** 6 servings (2 quarts).

Potatoes and roast beef come together in this rich and hearty soup. The result is a well-balanced, flavorful dish perfect for the fall.

**TASTE OF HOME
TEST KITCHEN**

meatball pizza subs

PREP/TOTAL TIME: 25 MIN.

1-1/3	cups pizza sauce
4	submarine buns, split and toasted
1-1/3	cups shredded part-skim mozzarella cheese
20	slices pepperoni
1	package (12 ounces) frozen fully cooked meatballs, thawed

Italian seasoning to taste

Spread 1/3 cup pizza sauce on the bottom of each bun. Top each with 1/3 cup cheese, five slices of pepperoni and three meatballs; sprinkle with Italian seasoning. Replace tops.

Wrap each sandwich in foil. Bake at 400° for 10-12 minutes or until heated through. **Yield:** 4 servings.

One busy weeknight, I created these quick and robust sandwiches with frozen meatballs and canned pizza sauce. They're a snap to prepare, and my family loves them!

ANN NOLTE
ELMENDORF AFB, ALASKA

 Easy Italian Seasoning: Don't make a special trip to the store when you see a recipe calls for Italian seasoning. You can blend just a few dried herbs with good results. Try substituting 1/4 teaspoon each of basil, thyme, rosemary and oregano for each teaspoon of Italian seasoning called for in a recipe.

cowboy chili

PREP/TOTAL TIME: 20 MIN.

1-1/2	cups refrigerated fully cooked barbecued shredded pork
1	can (14-1/2 ounces) diced tomatoes, undrained
1	cup canned black beans, rinsed and drained
3/4	cup beef broth
3/4	cup chopped green pepper
1/2	teaspoon minced garlic

In a large saucepan, combine all ingredients. Bring to a boil. Reduce the heat; simmer, uncovered, for 10-15 minutes or until heated through. **Yield:** 4 servings.

Sweet and chunky describe this great chili that kids will love. For the adults, add a dash or two of hot sauce and warm up your winter and your taste buds.

TASTE OF HOME
TEST KITCHEN

SOUPS & SANDWICHES

ramen corn chowder
PREP/TOTAL TIME: 15 MIN.

2	cups water
1	package (3 ounces) chicken ramen noodles
1	can (15-1/4 ounces) whole kernel corn, drained
1	can (14-3/4 ounces) cream-style corn
1	cup milk
1	teaspoon dried minced onion
1/4	teaspoon curry powder
3/4	cup shredded cheddar cheese
1	tablespoon crumbled cooked bacon
1	tablespoon minced fresh parsley

In a small saucepan, bring water to a boil. Break noodles into large pieces. Add noodles and contents of seasoning packet to water. Reduce heat to medium. Cook, uncovered, for 2-3 minutes or until noodles are tender.

Stir in the corn, cream-style corn, milk, onion and curry; heat through. Stir in the cheese, bacon and parsley until blended. **Yield:** 4 servings.

This chowder tastes as good as if it simmered for hours, but it's ready in 15 minutes. I thought the original recipe was lacking in flavor, so I jazzed it up with extra corn and bacon bits.

**DARLENE BRENDEN
SALEM, OREGON**

pizza sandwiches

PREP/TOTAL TIME: 20 MIN.

8	slices Italian bread (3/4 inch thick)
8	slices part-skim mozzarella cheese
8	slices tomato
4	teaspoons grated Parmesan cheese
1/4	teaspoon garlic salt
24	slices pepperoni
1/4	cup butter, softened

Pizza sauce, warmed

On four slices of bread, layer one slice of mozzarella, two slices of tomato, 1 teaspoon Parmesan cheese, a dash of garlic salt and six slices pepperoni. Top with remaining mozzarella and bread. Spread outside of sandwiches with butter.

On a hot griddle, toast sandwiches for 3-4 minutes on each side or until golden brown. Serve with pizza sauce. **Yield:** 4 servings.

I give grilled cheese a special treatment by using slices of mozzarella cheese and adding delicious extras like pepperoni and fresh tomatoes. Dipped in warm pizza sauce, each one will be a fast favorite!

MARY MONACO
COLUMBUS, OHIO

 Panini Press: Pizza Sandwiches can also be made on a panini press. Avoid bread slices that are too thick or too thin. Slices that are half an inch thick will withstand the grilling nicely.

SOUPS & SANDWICHES

 tuna melt on corn bread

PREP/TOTAL TIME: 30 MIN.

1	package (8-1/2 ounces) corn bread/muffin mix
2	cans (6 ounces *each*) light water-packed tuna, drained and flaked
1/3	cup mayonnaise
1/3	cup chopped celery
2	tablespoons finely chopped onion
1	hard-cooked egg, chopped
1	teaspoon dill weed
1/4	teaspoon salt
1/8	teaspoon pepper
6	slices cheddar cheese
1	medium tomato, sliced
1	medium ripe avocado, peeled and sliced

Prepare and bake corn bread according to package directions, using a greased 8-in. square baking pan. Cool on a wire rack.

In a small bowl, combine tuna, mayonnaise, celery, onion, egg, dill, salt and pepper. Cut corn bread into six pieces; place on an ungreased baking sheet. Top each with 1/4 cup tuna mixture and a slice of cheese.

Broil 4-6 in. from the heat for 2-3 minutes or until cheese is melted. Top with tomato and avocado. **Yield:** 6 servings.

Try a new taste for an open-faced tuna melt— serve it on corn bread for a quick lunch or dinner.

TASTE OF HOME TEST KITCHEN

 Plan Ahead: If you're anticipating a busy day, make the corn bread and tuna salad the night before. Store the bread in an airtight container at room temperature and chill the salad. Assemble and broil these sandwiches when ready to eat.

SOUPS & SANDWICHES

zucchini bisque

PREP/TOTAL TIME: 30 MIN.

4	medium zucchini, shredded
1	medium onion, chopped
1/2	cup butter, cubed
2-1/2	cups chicken broth
1	cup heavy whipping cream
3/4	teaspoon salt
1/2	teaspoon minced fresh basil
1/2	teaspoon pepper
1/4	teaspoon ground nutmeg

Sour cream and additional nutmeg, optional

In a large saucepan, saute zucchini and onion in butter for 5-6 minutes or until tender. Stir in broth. Bring to a boil. Reduce heat; cover and simmer for 12-15 minutes. Cool slightly.

Transfer to a food processor; cover and process on low until smooth. Return to the pan. Stir in the cream, salt, basil, pepper and nutmeg. Bring to a boil. Reduce heat; simmer, uncovered, for 1-2 minutes or until heated through. Garnish with sour cream and additional nutmeg if desired. **Yield:** 6 servings.

Looking for a different way to serve a bounty of zucchini? Try this soup! A food processor hurries along preparation of the thick, full-flavored blend that's accented by just a hint of nutmeg.

**GERMAINE STANK
POUND, WISCONSIN**

SOUPS & SANDWICHES

golden potato soup

PREP/TOTAL TIME: 30 MIN.

1	tablespoon butter
1	tablespoon canola oil
3	medium potatoes, peeled and cubed
1/2	teaspoon garlic salt
1/8	teaspoon pepper
1	can (14-1/2 ounces) chicken broth
1	small onion, chopped
1/4	cup crumbled cooked bacon
1	garlic clove, minced
1	teaspoon dried rosemary, crushed
1	teaspoon dried thyme
1	cup hot water

2	teaspoons chicken bouillon granules
1	cup heavy whipping cream
1/2	cup shredded cheddar cheese

In a large saucepan, heat butter and oil until butter is melted. Add the potatoes, garlic salt and pepper. Cook over medium heat for 4-6 minutes or until potatoes are tender and lightly browned.

Stir in the broth, onion, bacon, garlic, rosemary and thyme. Bring to a boil. Reduce heat; cover and simmer for 15 minutes. Stir in water and bouillon. Gradually stir in cream; heat through. Add cheese, stirring until melted. **Yield:** 4-1/2 cups.

Filled with flavor, herbs and potatoes, this warmer-upper soup is pure comfort food. It's one of my husband's very favorite cold-weather meals.

SHEILA HARMS
BATTLE LAKE, MINNESOTA

provolone burgers

PREP/TOTAL TIME: 25 MIN.

1	medium onion, finely chopped
2	eggs, lightly beaten
3	teaspoons dried basil
2	garlic cloves, minced
1	teaspoon dried oregano
1/2	teaspoon salt
1/4	teaspoon pepper
3	pounds ground beef
8	slices provolone cheese
8	sandwich rolls, split

Lettuce leaves

In a large bowl, combine the first seven ingredients. Crumble beef over mixture and mix well. Shape into eight patties.

Grill, covered, over medium-hot heat for 5-7 minutes on each side or until a meat thermometer reaches 160°.

Top each patty with a cheese slice; grill 1 minute more or until cheese is melted. Grill rolls cut side down for 1-2 minutes or until toasted. Top each with lettuce and a burger. **Yield:** 8 servings.

Grilled hamburgers that are seasoned with garlic, onion and herbs and topped with melted cheese are a summertime staple for us. A nice change of pace from the usual American or cheddar, mild provolone cheese is great on these beef patties.

CHERYL MACZKO
EGLON, WEST VIRGINIA

tip **Mixing Hamburger Meat:** If you don't like getting your hands messy when mixing hamburger meat mixture, put the ingredients in a large resealable plastic bag, then mix. Or if you do use your hands, first dampen them with water and nothing will stick.

SOUPS & SANDWICHES

fast french dip sandwiches

PREP/TOTAL TIME: 10 MIN.

1	can (10-1/2 ounces) condensed French onion soup, undiluted
1/2	pound thinly sliced deli roast beef
1/3	cup water
4	slices provolone cheese
4	sandwich buns, split

In a 1-qt. microwave-safe bowl, combine the soup, beef and water. Cover and microwave on high for 3 minutes or until heated through.

Meanwhile, place a slice of cheese on each bun bottom. Broil 4-6 in. from the heat for 1 minute or until cheese is melted.

Using a slotted spoon, place beef on buns; replace tops. Serve with onion soup for dipping. **Yield:** 4 servings.

EDITOR'S NOTE: This recipe was tested in a 1,100-watt microwave.

I was looking for ways to use up leftover beef when I created this tasty sandwich. I enjoy dipping it in the onion soup.

KARRIE WAGNER
BARBERTON, OHIO

gumbo in a jiffy

PREP/TOTAL TIME: 20 MIN.

3	Italian sausage links, sliced
1	can (14-1/2 ounces) diced tomatoes with green peppers and onions, undrained
1	can (14-1/2 ounces) chicken broth
1/2	cup water
1	cup uncooked instant rice
1	can (7 ounces) whole kernel corn, drained

In a large saucepan, cook sausage until no longer pink; drain. Stir in the tomatoes, broth and water; bring to a boil. Stir in rice and corn; cover and remove from the heat. Let stand for 5 minutes. **Yield:** 6 servings.

This is a yummy dish. My husband loves the kick Italian sausage gives this quick gumbo, and it's such a cinch to throw together.

AMY FLACK
HOMER CITY, PENNSYLVANIA

 Freezing Soup:
Soups are great to make when you have time, then freeze for fast future meals. Here are some hints for freezing.

To cool soup quickly before freezing, place the kettle in a sink filled with ice water. When cool, transfer to airtight freezer-safe containers, leaving 1/4-in. headspace for expansion.

Most soups freeze nicely. The exceptions are soups made with cream and potatoes. Those are better when eaten fresh.

It's best to add pasta and rice to the soup when ready to eat, not before freezing.

To help retain their fantastic flavor, don't freeze soups for longer than 3 months.

Thaw soup completely in the refrigerator and reheat in a saucepan.

beef macaroni soup

PREP/TOTAL TIME: 25 MIN.

1	pound ground beef
2	cups frozen mixed vegetables
1	can (14-1/2 ounces) diced tomatoes, undrained
1	can (14-1/2 ounces) beef broth
1/4	teaspoon pepper
1/2	cup uncooked elbow macaroni

In a large saucepan, cook beef over medium heat until no longer pink; drain. Stir in the mixed vegetables, tomatoes, broth and pepper. Bring to a boil; add macaroni. Reduce heat; cover and simmer for 8-10 minutes or until the macaroni and vegetables are tender. **Yield:** 5 servings.

This is a simplified version of delicious vegetable beef soup. With beef, veggies and pasta, it's just as good as the original with a lot less fuss.

DEBRA BAKER
GREENVILLE, NORTH CAROLINA

SOUPS & SANDWICHES

 30 ⟩ **hot colby ham sandwiches**

PREP/TOTAL TIME: 30 MIN.

1/2	cup butter, melted
2	tablespoons prepared mustard
1	tablespoon dried minced onion
1	tablespoon poppy seeds
2	to 3 teaspoons sugar
8	hamburger buns, split
8	slices Colby cheese
16	thin slices deli ham (about 1 pound)
1-1/2	cups (6 ounces) shredded part-skim mozzarella cheese

In a small bowl, combine the butter, mustard, onion, poppy seeds and sugar. Place roll bottoms, cut side up, in an ungreased 15-in. x 10-in. x 1-in. baking pan. Top each with Colby cheese, ham and mozzarella. Brush with half of the butter mixture.

Replace roll tops. Brush with remaining butter mixture. Bake, uncovered, at 350° for 10-15 minutes or until cheese is melted. **Yield:** 15 servings.

This yummy recipe is a winner with friends and family. Not only are the warm sandwiches a snap to prepare, but they smell so good when baking that no can resist them. They are a staple at our get-togethers.

SHERRY CRENSHAW
FORT WORTH, TEXAS

blt's with raisin-avocado spread

PREP/TOTAL TIME: 20 MIN.

1	medium ripe avocado, peeled and cubed
4	ounces cream cheese, cubed
1/2	cup golden raisins
1/4	cup pine nuts
1/4	cup minced fresh parsley
1/2	teaspoon salt
1/4	teaspoon pepper
12	slices sourdough bread, toasted
12	bacon strips, cooked and halved
12	romaine leaves
6	slices tomato

In a food processor, combine the first seven ingredients; cover and process until blended. Spread evenly over six slices of toast. Layer with bacon, lettuce and tomato. Top with remaining toast. **Yield:** 6 servings.

If you're looking to dress up a bacon, lettuce and tomato sandwich, try spreading on a blend of cream cheese, avocado and raisins instead of mayonnaise.

VERONICA CALLAGHAN
GLASTONBURY, CONNECTICUT

Removing an Avocado Pit: Wash the avocado. Cut in half lengthwise, cutting around the seed. Twist halves in opposite directions to separate. Slip a tablespoon under the seed to loosen it from the fruit. To remove avocado flesh from the skin, loosen it from the skin with a large spoon and scoop out. Slice the peeled avocado as desired. Or cut into unpeeled wedges and slice between the flesh and the skin.

beer cheese soup

PREP/TOTAL TIME: 20 MIN.

2	tablespoons finely chopped onion
1/2	teaspoon butter
2	cans (10-3/4 ounces *each*) condensed cream of celery soup, undiluted
1	cup beer *or* nonalcoholic beer
1	cup milk
1	teaspoon Worcestershire sauce
1/2	teaspoon dried parsley flakes
1/4	teaspoon paprika
3/4	pound process cheese (Velveeta), cubed

In a large saucepan, saute onion in butter. Stir in the soup, beer, milk, Worcestershire sauce, parsley and paprika. Reduce heat; stir in cheese until melted. Heat through (do not boil). **Yield:** 6 servings.

Onion, parsley, paprika and beer flavor this smooth, rich soup. A family friend used to invite us over for Sunday supper and served this several times. I just had to get the recipe.

SHARON LOCK
FORMAN, NORTH DAKOTA

SOUPS & SANDWICHES

 beefy bean soup

PREP/TOTAL TIME: 30 MIN.

1	can (29 ounces) tomato puree
1	can (14-1/2 ounces) diced tomatoes, undrained
1	cup water
1	cup beef broth
4-1/2	teaspoons chicken bouillon granules
3/4	teaspoon salt
3/4	teaspoon dried basil
3/4	teaspoon dried oregano
3/4	cup uncooked elbow macaroni
1/2	pound ground beef
1	cup chopped celery
1/2	cup chopped onion
1/2	teaspoon dried minced garlic
1	can (16 ounces) kidney beans, rinsed and drained
1	can (15-1/2 ounces) great northern beans, rinsed and drained

In a Dutch oven, combine the first eight ingredients. Bring to a boil. Stir in macaroni. Reduce heat; simmer, uncovered, for 10-15 minutes or until macaroni is tender.

Meanwhile, in a large skillet, cook the beef, celery, onion and garlic over medium heat until meat is no longer pink and vegetables are tender; drain. Add to the tomato mixture. Stir in beans; heat through. **Yield:** 8 servings (3 quarts).

This quick and filling soup makes a bunch, but it won't last long! Any leftovers are even better the next day.

CAROLYN BURBIDGE
BOUNTIFUL, UTAH

Buy in Bulk:
It's more economical to buy ground beef in 3-pound packages. When you get home, divide the package into 1/2- or 1-pound portions to freeze for use in soups, casseroles, hamburgers and meatballs.

italian meatball sandwiches

30

PREP/TOTAL TIME: 25 MIN.

2	packages (12 ounces *each*) frozen Italian meatballs
1	jar (28 ounces) spaghetti sauce
3/4	cup sliced fresh mushrooms
3/4	cup chopped green pepper
6	hoagie *or* submarine buns, split

Place meatballs in a microwave-safe dish. Cover and microwave on high for 1-2 minutes or until slightly thawed.

Transfer to a large saucepan; add the spaghetti sauce, mushrooms and green pepper. Bring to a boil. Reduce heat; simmer, uncovered, for 3-6 minutes or until the meatballs are heated through. Serve on buns. **Yield:** 6 servings.

EDITOR'S NOTE: This recipe was tested in a 1,100-watt microwave.

Frozen meatballs and store-bought spaghetti sauce are the time-saving tricks to these fast and satisfying sandwiches. Whip them up and watch them disappear!

TASTE OF HOME
TEST KITCHEN

SOUPS & SANDWICHES

turkey meatball soup

PREP/TOTAL TIME: 30 MIN.

1 package (12 ounces) refrigerated fully cooked Italian turkey meatballs
1 can (49-1/2 ounces) chicken broth
2 cups uncooked egg noodles
2 cups cut fresh green beans
1 cup sliced fresh carrots
1 cup chopped celery
1 cup chopped onion
1 tablespoon dried parsley flakes
1 teaspoon garlic powder
1 teaspoon dried oregano
1 teaspoon dried basil
1/4 teaspoon pepper

In a Dutch oven, combine all ingredients. Bring to a boil. Reduce heat; simmer, uncovered, for 20-25 minutes or until noodles are tender. **Yield:** 6 servings.

Fresh green beans and carrots add color and a boost of nutrition to hearty meatball noodle soup.

**TASTE OF HOME
TEST KITCHEN**

Ingredient Idea: Cooked Italian turkey meatballs can be found in the refrigerated section of your local grocery store. You can substitute frozen beef meatballs.

corny ham bundles

PREP/TOTAL TIME: 30 MIN.

30

1	package (3 ounces) cream cheese, softened
1	tablespoon mayonnaise
1/2	teaspoon ground mustard
1/4	teaspoon celery seed
1	cup cubed fully cooked ham
1/2	cup fresh *or* frozen corn
1/4	cup shredded Monterey Jack cheese
2	teaspoons finely chopped onion
1	tube (8 ounces) refrigerated crescent rolls
1	tablespoon butter, melted
1	tablespoon finely crushed corn chips

In a small bowl, beat the cream cheese, mayonnaise, mustard and celery seed until blended. Stir in the ham, corn, cheese and onion. Unroll crescent roll dough and separate into four rectangles; seal perforations.

Spoon about 1/2 cup ham mixture into the center of each rectangle. Bring edges up to the center and pinch to seal. Brush with butter; sprinkle with corn chips.

Transfer to an ungreased baking sheet. Bake at 375° for 15-20 minutes or until golden brown. **Yield:** 4 servings.

These savory little sandwiches taste great, use up leftover ham and come together easily with a tube of refrigerated crescent rolls.

SANDY DEMARS
CROWN POINT, INDIANA

SOUPS & SANDWICHES

 ## basil chicken sandwiches

PREP/TOTAL TIME: 15 MIN.

1/2	teaspoon pepper
1/4	teaspoon salt
Dash paprika	
1	pound boneless skinless chicken breasts, cut into 1/2-inch slices
6	tablespoons prepared olive oil vinaigrette salad dressing, *divided*
6	Italian *or* French sandwich rolls, split
18	basil leaves
1	jar (7 ounces) roasted sweet red peppers, drained
1/4	cup shredded Romano cheese

In a bowl, combine the pepper, salt and paprika; sprinkle over chicken slices. In a nonstick skillet over medium-high heat, cook chicken in 2 tablespoons salad dressing for 4-5 minutes on each side or until chicken is no longer pink.

Brush remaining salad dressing on rolls. Place basil leaves on rolls; top with chicken and red peppers. Sprinkle with Romano cheese. **Yield:** 6 servings.

I got the inspiration for this recipe when family members with food allergies were coming to see our new home. I created this chicken sandwich with fresh basil for our lunch.

KERRY DURGIN KREBS
NEW MARKET, MARYLAND

Say 'Bye to Basil: Some family members may not care for the flavor of basil in these grilled chicken sandwiches. You can replace some or all of the robust herb with any kind of lettuce or even spinach leaves.

reuben crescents

PREP/TOTAL TIME: 20 MIN.

20

1 tube (8 ounces) refrigerated crescent rolls
1 cup sauerkraut, rinsed, well drained and chopped
1 tablespoon Thousand Island salad dressing
4 slices process Swiss cheese, cut into 1/2-inch strips
8 thin slices deli corned beef

Separate crescent dough into eight triangles. In a small bowl, combine sauerkraut and salad dressing.

Place two cheese strips across the short side of each triangle. Fold corned beef slices in half; place over cheese. Top with sauerkraut mixture. Roll up each from the short side.

Place on an ungreased baking sheet. Bake at 375° for 10-15 minutes or until golden brown. **Yield:** 8 servings.

If you like Reuben sandwiches, you're sure to like these quick-and-easy roll-ups. I serve them with a salad and some fruit for a fast meal.

DOLORES HURTT
FLORENCE, MONTANA

SOUPS & SANDWICHES

creamy chicken rice soup

PREP/TOTAL TIME: 30 MIN.

1/2	cup chopped onion
1	medium carrot, chopped
1	celery rib, chopped
1	tablespoon canola oil
1/2	teaspoon minced garlic
2	cans (14-1/2 ounces *each*) chicken broth
1/3	cup uncooked long grain rice
3/4	teaspoon dried basil
1/4	teaspoon pepper
3	tablespoons all-purpose flour
1	can (5 ounces) evaporated milk
1	package (9 ounces) frozen diced cooked chicken, thawed

In a large saucepan, saute the onion, carrot and celery in oil until tender. Add garlic; cook 1 minute longer. Stir in the broth, rice, basil and pepper. Bring to a boil. Reduce heat; cover and simmer for 15 minutes or until rice is tender.

In a small bowl, combine flour and milk until smooth; stir into soup. Bring to a boil; cook and stir for 2 minutes or until thickened. Stir in chicken; heat through. **Yield:** 5 servings.

I came up with this thick, flavorful soup while making some adjustments to a favorite stovetop chicken casserole. It goes together in short order using precooked chicken chunks and a couple of pulses in a mini-processor to chop the veggies.

JANICE MITCHELL
AURORA, COLORADO

Choice Chicken: You can replace the frozen diced cooked chicken with 2 cups cubed chicken left over from your Sunday dinner.

pizza burgers

PREP/TOTAL TIME: 30 MIN.

1	can (6 ounces) tomato paste
1/2	teaspoon salt
1/2	teaspoon dried oregano
1/4	teaspoon garlic salt
1/4	teaspoon pepper
1/4	teaspoon aniseed
1-1/2	pounds lean ground beef
1/2	cup shredded part-skim mozzarella cheese
6	hamburger buns, split
6	lettuce leaves
6	tomato slices

In a large bowl, combine the first six ingredients. Crumble beef over mixture; mix well. Shape into six patties. Place on broiler pan coated with cooking spray.

Broil 6 in. from heat for 5-6 minutes on each side or until juices run clear. Sprinkle with cheese. Broil 1 minute longer or until cheese is melted. Serve on buns with lettuce and tomato. **Yield:** 6 servings.

This better-for-you version of an all-time lunch counter classic is loaded with popular pizza flavor. The cheese-topped burgers are also fast to fix.

LISA TRUCKENBROD
BELOIT, WISCONSIN

creamy tomato basil soup

PREP/TOTAL TIME: 25 MIN.

2	tablespoons chopped green onion
2	garlic cloves, minced
1-1/2	teaspoons olive oil
1	can (28 ounces) crushed tomatoes
1	can (10-1/2 ounces) condensed chicken broth, undiluted
1-1/3	cups water
1/4	teaspoon pepper
3/4	cup heavy whipping cream
2	tablespoons sherry *or* additional chicken broth
2	tablespoons minced fresh basil
2	teaspoons sugar

In a large saucepan, saute onion and garlic in oil until tender. Add the tomatoes, broth, water and pepper. Bring to a boil. Reduce heat; simmer for 10 minutes.

Stir in the cream, sherry or additional broth, basil and sugar. Cook for 1 minute or until heated through (do not boil). **Yield:** 6 servings.

I created this soup in an attempt to duplicate one I enjoyed at a restaurant in Philadelphia. My husband and I love this on cold nights with a grilled cheese sandwich. It's so easy to make.

LINDA MANUSZAK
CLINTON TOWNSHIP, MICHIGAN

turkey burgers with jalapeno cheese sauce

PREP/TOTAL TIME: 25 MIN.

3	slices whole wheat bread, torn
1	cup milk, *divided*
6	garlic cloves, minced
1-1/2	teaspoons ground mustard
1/4	teaspoon salt
1/4	teaspoon pepper
1-1/2	pounds lean ground turkey
1-1/4	teaspoons all-purpose flour
3/4	cup shredded cheddar cheese
1	jalapeno pepper, seeded and chopped
6	whole wheat hamburger buns, split
6	lettuce leaves
6	slices tomato

In a large bowl, soak bread in 1/2 cup milk for 1 minute. Add the garlic, mustard, salt and pepper. Crumble turkey over mixture and mix well. Shape into six patties; set aside.

In a small saucepan, combine the flour and remaining milk until smooth. Bring to a boil; cook and stir for 1-2 minutes or until thickened. Remove from the heat. Add cheese and jalapeno; stir until cheese is melted. Keep warm.

Coat grill rack with cooking spray before starting the grill. Grill patties, covered, over medium heat for 5-7 minutes on each side or until a meat thermometer reads 165° and juices run clear. Serve on buns with the lettuce, tomato and jalapeno cheese sauce. **Yield:** 6 servings.

EDITOR'S NOTE: When cutting hot peppers, disposable gloves are recommended. Avoid touching your face.

This is a lighter version of a tasty burger that people enjoyed at a place I once worked. I substituted the beef with turkey and used low-fat cheese, but the results are tastier than the original crowd-pleaser.

**VICKI SCHURK
HAMDEN, CONNECTICUT**

Cool as a Cucumber: Balance the heat from these burgers by serving a crisp cucumber salad on the side.

ham and bean soup

30>

PREP/TOTAL TIME: 30 MIN.

2   medium carrots, sliced
2   celery ribs, chopped
1/2   cup chopped onion
2   tablespoons butter
4   cans (15-1/2 ounces *each*) great northern beans, rinsed and drained
4   cups chicken broth
2   cups cubed fully cooked ham
1   teaspoon chili powder
1/2   teaspoon minced garlic
1/4   teaspoon pepper
1   bay leaf

In a large saucepan, saute the carrots, celery and onion in butter until tender. Stir in the remaining ingredients. Bring to a boil. Reduce heat; cook for 15 minutes or until heated through. Discard bay leaf. **Yield:** 7 servings.

If you like ham and bean soup but don't want to spend hours in the kitchen, this tasty and timely version will leave you with a satisfied smile.

TASTE OF HOME
TEST KITCHEN

SOUPS & SANDWICHES

 30 ## macaroni vegetable soup

PREP/TOTAL TIME: 30 MIN.

1	medium zucchini, julienned
1/2	cup finely chopped onion
1	medium carrot, halved and thinly sliced
1	tablespoon butter
2	cans (14-1/2 ounces *each*) chicken broth
1	cup tomato *or* vegetable juice
1/2	cup uncooked elbow macaroni
1/8	to 1/4 teaspoon cayenne pepper
1	can (15 ounces) white kidney *or* cannellini beans, rinsed and drained
1/2	cup frozen corn

In a large saucepan, saute the zucchini, onion and carrot in butter until tender. Add broth and tomato juice. Bring to a boil; stir in macaroni and cayenne. Cook for 10 minutes or until macaroni is tender. Stir in the beans and corn; heat through. **Yield:** 8 servings (2 quarts).

Colorful veggie soup with a hint of cayenne is a nice change of pace from heavy cream soups. The hearty yet healthy combination can be served as a side dish or light meal.

**EDNA HOFFMAN
HEBRON, INDIANA**

Turn Up the Heat:
Perk up the flavor of Macaroni Vegetable Soup by using the higher range of cayenne pepper (1/4 teaspoon) and by replacing the tomato juice with spicy vegetable juice.

pesto hamburgers

PREP/TOTAL TIME: 20 MIN.

20>

1-1/2	pounds ground beef
1/8	teaspoon salt
1/8	teaspoon pepper
4	slices part-skim mozzarella cheese
1/2	cup prepared pesto
1/3	cup roasted sweet red pepper strips
4	hamburger buns, split and toasted

Shape beef into four 3/4-in.-thick patties. Season with salt and pepper. In a large skillet, cook patties over medium heat for 5 minutes on each side or until meat is no longer pink.

Top each burger with one slice of cheese, 2 tablespoons pesto and pepper strips. Reduce the heat; cover and simmer for 2 minutes or until cheese melts. Serve on buns. **Yield:** 4 servings.

Give an Italian twist to basic burgers by topping them with pesto, roasted red peppers strips and mozzarella cheese.

**TASTE OF HOME
TEST KITCHEN**

SOUPS & SANDWICHES

 dilled cajun chicken sandwiches

PREP/TOTAL TIME: 25 MIN.

4	boneless skinless chicken breast halves (4 ounces *each*)
3	tablespoons olive oil
2	tablespoons Cajun seasoning
1/4	cup mayonnaise
2	teaspoons dill weed
1	teaspoon minced garlic
4	sandwich rolls, split
4	lettuce leaves
4	slices tomato
4	slices provolone cheese

Flatten chicken to 1/4-in. thickness. In a large skillet, combine the olive oil and Cajun seasoning; add chicken and turn to coat. Cook, uncovered, over medium heat for 5-6 minutes on each side or until no longer pink.

Meanwhile, in a small bowl, combine the mayonnaise, dill and garlic. Spread over cut sides of rolls. On roll bottoms, layer the lettuce, tomato, cheese and chicken; replace roll tops. **Yield:** 4 servings.

I came up with this recipe when my husband and I were looking for something quick. We both love Cajun seasoning, and the same goes for garlic and dill. We combined them in these delicious sandwiches.

ABBY TEEL
BOISE, IDAHO

jack 'n' jill burgers

PREP/TOTAL TIME: 30 MIN.

30

1	medium onion
1/2	cup finely crushed seasoned salad croutons
1/4	cup dill pickle relish
2	tablespoons ketchup
1-1/2	pounds ground beef
6	slices Monterey Jack cheese
6	hamburger buns, split
6	lettuce leaves
6	slices tomato

In a large bowl, combine the first four ingredients. Crumble beef over the mixture and mix well. Shape into six 1/2-in. thick patties; place on an ungreased broiler pan.

Broil 4 in. from the heat for 7-9 minutes on each side or until no longer pink. Top each with a cheese slice. Broil 1-2 minutes longer or until cheese is melted. Serve on buns with lettuce and tomato slices. **Yield:** 6 servings.

Whether or not family members spent the day fetching pails of water, they're sure to fall for these speedy sandwiches.

TASTE OF HOME
TEST KITCHEN

Homemade Tortilla Chips: Serve these burgers with tortilla star snacks. Brush both sides of six 10-inch flour tortillas with 3 tablespoons melted butter. Combine 1/2 teaspoon dried basil, 1/2 teaspoon dried thyme, 1/4 teaspoon seasoned salt, 1/4 teaspoon garlic powder and 1/8 teaspoon pepper; sprinkle over one side of each tortilla. With a 2-1/2-in. star-shaped cookie cutter, cut out several stars from each tortilla; discard scraps. Place stars on ungreased baking sheets. Bake at 400° for 7-9 minutes or until crisp.

SOUPS & SANDWICHES

30 reuben chowder

PREP/TOTAL TIME: 25 MIN.

1	small onion, sliced
1	tablespoon canola oil
2	cans (14-1/2 ounces *each*) vegetable broth
1	can (14-1/2 ounces) beef broth
2	teaspoons prepared horseradish
1	teaspoon Worcestershire sauce
1/2	teaspoon ground mustard
1/4	teaspoon celery salt
5	ounces deli corned beef, chopped
1	cup sauerkraut, rinsed and well drained
2	slices rye bread, cubed
4	slices Swiss cheese

In a small skillet, saute onion in oil until tender. Meanwhile, in a large saucepan, bring the vegetable and beef broths to a boil; stir in the horseradish, Worcestershire sauce, mustard and celery salt. Add the corned beef, sauerkraut and onion. Reduce heat to low; cover and simmer for 10 minutes.

Ladle soup into four ovenproof bowls; top with bread cubes and Swiss cheese. Broil 3-4 in. from heat for 2-3 minutes or until cheese is melted. **Yield:** 4 servings.

This dish contains all of your favorite Reuben sandwich ingredients in a delicious soup. If you don't have bread, simply cut the Swiss cheese into strips and place it on the broth.

**TASTE OF HOME
TEST KITCHEN**

fiery spinach chicken salad, pg. 156

SALADS & SIDES

SALADS & SIDES

 grape tomato mozzarella salad

PREP/TOTAL TIME: 15 MIN.

1/2	large sweet onion, thinly sliced
1	medium cucumber, sliced
2	cups grape tomatoes
1/2	cup loosely packed fresh basil leaves, sliced
4	ounces fresh mozzarella cheese, sliced
1/3	cup Italian salad dressing

Arrange the onion, cucumber, tomatoes, basil and mozzarella on salad plates. Drizzle with dressing. Serve immediately. **Yield:** 6 servings.

I created this fuss-free recipe after tasting something similar on a cruise. It makes a speedy, summery light bite.

LINDA HAAS
TENMILE, OREGON

Quickly Cut Basil:
To quickly chop a lot of basil, first sprinkle a few drops of vegetable oil on the leaves and gently rub to evenly coat the leaves. This will prevent them from darkening. Stack several basil leaves; roll into a tight tube. Slice the leaves widthwise into narrow pieces to create long thin strips. If you'd like smaller pieces, simply chop the strips.

artichoke turkey salami salad

PREP: 20 MIN. + CHILLING

4   cups cooked elbow macaroni
2   cups (8 ounces) shredded part-skim mozzarella cheese
2   cups cherry tomatoes, halved
8   ounces turkey salami, cut into thin strips
1   cup roasted sweet red pepper strips, drained
1   jar (7-1/2 ounces) marinated artichoke hearts, drained and chopped
1   can (2-1/4 ounces) sliced ripe olives, drained

1/3   cup Italian salad dressing
1/4   cup minced fresh basil
1/2   teaspoon pepper

In a large salad bowl, combine the macaroni, mozzarella, tomatoes, salami, red peppers, artichokes and olives. Add the dressing, basil and pepper; toss to coat.

Cover and refrigerate for 2 hours or overnight. Toss before serving. **Yield:** 8 servings.

This pasta salad chills for 2 hours, allowing the flavors to blend. Plus, it means no last-minute fuss at dinnertime!

TASTE OF HOME
TEST KITCHEN

SALADS & SIDES

mushroom rice

PREP/TOTAL TIME: 25 MIN.

1	small onion, finely chopped
1	celery rib, chopped
1/2	cup chopped celery leaves
2	tablespoons butter
1	pound sliced fresh mushrooms
3	cups uncooked instant rice
3	cups water
4	teaspoons Greek seasoning
1/2	cup chopped pecans, toasted

In a large nonstick skillet coated with cooking spray, saute the onion, celery and celery leaves in butter for 4 minutes. Add mushrooms; cook 4 minutes longer.

Add rice; cook for 4-5 minutes or until lightly browned. Stir in the water and Greek seasoning. Bring to a boil. Remove from the heat; cover and let stand for 5 minutes. Fluff rice with a fork. Sprinkle with the pecans. **Yield:** 8 servings.

Don't count on having any leftovers with this delicious, simple dish. A friend gave me the recipe more than a decade ago, and it's been a family favorite ever since.

BETH MCCAW
NASHVILLE, TENNESSEE

Homemade Greek Seasoning:
To make 2 tablespoons Greek seasoning, combine the following:
1-1/2 teaspoons dried oregano, 1 teaspoon dried mint, 1 teaspoon dried thyme, 1/2 teaspoon dried basil, 1/2 teaspoon dried marjoram, 1/2 teaspoon dried minced onion and 1/4 teaspoon dried minced garlic. Store in an airtight container in a cool, dry place for up to 6 months.

lazy days potato salad

PREP/TOTAL TIME: 20 MIN.

1	can (14-1/2 ounces) sliced potatoes, drained
1/4	cup thinly sliced celery
1/4	cup sliced green onions
1/4	cup shredded carrot
1	can (2-1/4 ounces) sliced ripe olives, drained
2	tablespoons chopped dill pickle
1/2	cup mayonnaise
1	to 2 tablespoons Dijon mustard
1/4	teaspoon garlic powder
1/4	teaspoon pepper

In a large bowl, combine first six ingredients. In a small bowl, combine the mayonnaise, mustard, garlic powder and pepper. Drizzle over the potato mixture and toss to coat. Cover and refrigerate until serving. **Yield:** 4 servings.

I cut the prep time for homemade potato salad to almost nothing by using canned potatoes. Slice in some crunchy veggies and diced dill pickles and then drizzle with a light creamy dressing seasoned with garlic and mustard.

MARGARET WILSON
SUN CITY, CALIFORNIA

SALADS & SIDES

floret pasta toss

PREP/TOTAL TIME: 20 MIN.

8	ounces uncooked penne pasta
1-1/2	cups fresh cauliflowerets
1-1/2	cups fresh broccoli florets
2	small tomatoes, seeded and chopped
1	small onion, sliced
1/2	cup Italian salad dressing
2	to 3 tablespoons balsamic vinegar
1/4	teaspoon salt
1/8	teaspoon pepper

Cook pasta according to package directions. Meanwhile, in a large bowl, combine the cauliflower, broccoli, tomatoes and onion.

In a small bowl, whisk the salad dressing, vinegar, salt and pepper. Drain pasta and rinse in cold water; add to vegetable mixture. Drizzle with dressing and toss to coat. Chill until serving. **Yield:** 9 servings.

This refreshing salad is fast to prepare because you can cut the vegetables while the pasta cooks. I just threw it together, adding flavors that suited my taste buds. Feel free to add a few of your own.

KARI CONGENIE
OAKBROOK TERRACE, ILLINOIS

SALADS & SIDES

colorful tomato 'n' mozzarella salad

PREP: 20 MIN. + STANDING

1	cup fresh baby spinach
2	medium yellow tomatoes, sliced
2	medium red tomatoes, sliced
4	ounces fresh mozzarella cheese, sliced
2	tablespoons thinly sliced fresh basil leaves
1/4	teaspoon salt
1/4	teaspoon pepper
1	tablespoon balsamic vinegar
2	teaspoons olive oil

Arrange spinach on a platter; top with tomatoes and cheese slices. Sprinkle with basil, salt and pepper. Drizzle with vinegar and oil. Let stand for 15 minutes before serving. **Yield:** 4 servings.

This is my twist on the popular tomato-mozzarella salad. Since the rest of the salad is so light, you can splurge with the fresh mozzarella!

TARI AMBLER
SHOREWOOD, ILLINOIS

In-A-Dash Dressing:
The vinegar and oil dressing in this recipe comes together in no time. But feel free to use bottled vinaigrette if you have some in the fridge to use up.

garbanzo bean medley

PREP/TOTAL TIME: 10 MIN.

1	small zucchini, cubed
1	teaspoon olive oil
2	teaspoons minced garlic
1	can (15 ounces) garbanzo beans *or* chickpeas, rinsed and drained
1	can (14-1/2 ounces) diced tomatoes, undrained
1	teaspoon Italian seasoning
1/4	teaspoon crushed red pepper flakes, optional
1/4	cup shredded Parmesan cheese

In a small skillet, saute zucchini in oil until tender. Add garlic; saute 1 minute longer. Stir in the garbanzo beans, tomatoes, Italian seasoning and pepper flakes if desired; heat through. Sprinkle with Parmesan cheese. **Yield:** 4 servings.

I'm a vegetarian looking for tasty dishes without meat. This Italian bean recipe is fast, flavorful and filling. Sprinkle feta cheese on top for a change of pace.

DENISE NEAL
YORBA LINDA, CALIFORNIA

SALADS & SIDES

grilled chicken caesar salad

PREP: 15 MIN. + MARINATING GRILL: 15 MIN.

1/2	cup red wine vinegar
1/2	cup soy sauce
1/2	cup olive oil
1	tablespoon dried parsley flakes
1	teaspoon dried basil
1	teaspoon dried oregano
1/2	teaspoon garlic powder
1/2	teaspoon pepper
6	boneless skinless chicken breast halves (4 ounces *each*)
1	large bunch romaine, torn (12 cups)
1-1/2	cups Caesar salad croutons
1	cup halved cherry tomatoes
2/3	cup creamy Caesar salad dressing

In a large resealable plastic bag, combine the first eight ingredients; add the chicken. Seal bag and turn to coat; refrigerate for at least 4 hours.

Drain and discard marinade. Grill chicken, uncovered, over medium-low heat for 6-8 minutes on each side or until a meat thermometer reads 170°.

Meanwhile, in a large bowl, combine the romaine, croutons and tomatoes; add the dressing and toss to coat. Divide among six salad plates. Slice chicken; arrange on salads. **Yield:** 6 servings.

Whenever we're invited to potlucks, I'm always asked to bring a salad because people know it's one of my specialties. This dish is especially good on summer days when it's too hot to cook on the stove.

DEB WEISBERGER
MULLET LAKE, MICHIGAN

speedy spanish rice

PREP/TOTAL TIME: 25 MIN.

1-1/2	cups uncooked instant brown rice
1	medium onion, chopped
1	small green pepper, chopped
1	garlic clove, minced
1	tablespoon butter
1-1/2	cups water
1	tablespoon minced fresh cilantro
2	teaspoons ground cumin
1-1/2	teaspoons chicken bouillon granules
1/4	teaspoon pepper
1	cup picante sauce

In a large nonstick skillet, saute the rice, onion, green pepper and garlic in butter until rice is lightly browned and vegetables are crisp-tender. Stir in the water, cilantro, cumin, bouillon and pepper; bring to a boil. Reduce the heat; cover and simmer for 5 minutes.

Remove from the heat; let stand for 5 minutes. Fluff with a fork. Stir in the picante sauce. **Yield:** 4 servings.

Mexican food is big with our family. In fact, one of my nephews loves this dish so much that he always requests it for his special birthday dinner!

ANGIE RORICK
FORT WAYNE, INDIANA

 Prefer Parsley? Cilantro can add a distinctive, slightly sharp flavor to Mexican dishes. If you and your family don't care for the taste, use parsley instead.

SALADS & SIDES

fiery chicken spinach salad

PREP/TOTAL TIME: 10 MIN.

6	frozen breaded spicy chicken breast strips, thawed
1	package (6 ounces) fresh baby spinach
1	medium tomato, cut into 12 wedges
1/2	cup chopped green pepper
1/2	cup fresh baby carrots
1	can (15 ounces) black beans, rinsed and drained
1	can (11 ounces) Mexicorn, drained
3	tablespoons salsa
3	tablespoons barbecue sauce
3	tablespoons prepared ranch salad dressing
2	tablespoons shredded Mexican cheese blend

Heat chicken strips in a microwave according to package directions. Meanwhile, arrange the spinach on individual plates; top with tomato, green pepper, carrots, beans and corn.

In a small bowl, combine the salsa, barbecue sauce and ranch dressing. Place chicken over salads. Drizzle with dressing; sprinkle with cheese. **Yield:** 6 servings.

EDITOR'S NOTE: This recipe was tested in a 1,100-watt microwave.

This hearty and colorful main-course salad is easy to throw together when I get home from work, because it uses canned black beans and Mexicorn and packaged chicken breast strips. I sometimes add a can of ripe olives and garden-fresh cherry tomatoes.

KATI SPENCER
TAYLORSVILLE, UTAH

bruschetta polenta

PREP/TOTAL TIME: 10 MIN.

1 tube (1 pound) polenta, cut into 1/2-inch slices
1 tablespoon olive oil
1 cup bruschetta topping
3 tablespoons shredded Parmesan cheese

In a large skillet, cook polenta slices in oil over medium heat for 2 minutes on each side or until golden. Place the bruschetta topping in a microwave-safe bowl; cover and cook on high for 1 minute. Spoon 1 tablespoon of the bruschetta onto each slice of polenta; sprinkle with the Parmesan cheese. **Yield:** 6 servings.

EDITOR'S NOTE: Look for bruschetta topping in the pasta aisle or your grocer's deli case.

Serve tomato-topped polenta alongside your favorite soup. Or add cooked, crumbled Italian sausage and serve it as a main dish.

TASTE OF HOME TEST KITCHEN

Serving Suggestions: You can also use bruschetta to top slices of fresh French bread for an easy appetizer. Or toss it with hot cooked pasta for a marvelous meatless meal.

SALADS & SIDES

pecan brussels sprouts

PREP/TOTAL TIME: 15 MIN.

12   ounces fresh *or* frozen brussels sprouts (about 3 cups)
3   tablespoons water
1   cup pecan halves
2   tablespoons butter, melted
1/4   teaspoon salt
1/8   teaspoon pepper
1/8   teaspoon ground nutmeg

Trim brussels spouts and cut an X in the core of each. In a microwave-safe dish, combine the brussels sprouts and water. Cover and microwave on high for 3-4 minutes or until tender; drain. Add the pecans, butter, salt, pepper and nutmeg; toss to coat. **Yield:** 4 servings.

EDITOR'S NOTE: This recipe was tested in a 1,100-watt microwave.

Your family will eagerly eat their vegetables when you serve this dish. Crunchy pecans are a nice contrast to the tender brussels sprouts.

**TASTE OF HOME
TEST KITCHEN**

Brussels Basics:
The leaves of brussels sprouts cook faster than the core. To ensure even cooking, it's important to cut a deep X in the core of each sprout.

crab pasta salad

PREP: 30 MIN. + CHILLING

8	ounces uncooked spiral pasta
1	package (8 ounces) imitation crabmeat, chopped
1	cup frozen peas, thawed
1	cup fresh broccoli florets
1/2	cup chopped green pepper
1/4	cup sliced green onions
3/4	cup mayonnaise
1/3	cup Italian salad dressing
3	tablespoons grated Parmesan cheese

Cook pasta according to package directions; drain and rinse in cold water. In a large bowl, combine the pasta, crab, peas, broccoli, green pepper and onions. Combine the mayonnaise, salad dressing and Parmesan cheese; pour over pasta mixture and toss to coat. Cover and refrigerate for 2 hours or until chilled. **Yield:** 6 servings.

I also make this recipe with fat-free mayonnaise and reduced-fat dressing. Doing so doesn't affect the delightful flavor.

HEATHER O'NEILL
DUDLEY, MASSACHUSETTS

SALADS & SIDES

baked potatoes with topping
PREP/TOTAL TIME: 25 MIN.

6	large baking potatoes
1/3	cup butter, softened
6	green onions, sliced
1/4	cup mayonnaise
2	tablespoons crumbled cooked bacon
1-1/2	cups (6 ounces) shredded cheddar cheese

Scrub and pierce potatoes; place on a microwave-safe plate. Microwave, uncovered, on high for 20-23 minutes or until tender, turning once.

Meanwhile, in a small bowl, combine the butter, onions, mayonnaise and bacon; set aside. Cut an X in the top of each potato; fluff pulp with a fork. Top each with 3 tablespoons of the butter mixture. Sprinkle with the cheese. **Yield:** 6 servings.

EDITOR'S NOTE: This recipe was tested in a 1,100-watt microwave.

I jazz up baked potatoes with a rich topping. It's easy, fast and everyone really enjoys it. It makes potatoes a little more special.

**ALICE DEPAUW
DEFUNIAK SPRINGS
FLORIDA**

colorful vegetable medley

PREP/TOTAL TIME: 15 MIN.

20⟩

2	medium yellow summer squash, sliced
4	teaspoons olive oil
1-1/2	cups fresh sugar snap peas
1-1/2	cups halved cherry tomatoes
3	tablespoons minced fresh parsley
2	tablespoons lemon juice
1/2	teaspoon ground coriander
1/4	teaspoon salt
1/8	teaspoon pepper

In a large nonstick skillet, saute squash in oil for 3 minutes. Add peas and tomatoes; saute 2-3 minutes longer or until squash is crisp-tender. Sprinkle with the parsley, lemon juice, coriander, salt and pepper; toss to coat. **Yield:** 4 servings.

Here's a tasty way to get your daily veggies. We sprinkled this crisp-tender medley with fresh parsley, lemon juice and coriander. It's a quick side dish for any meal.

TASTE OF HOME
TEST KITCHEN

Squash Secrets: If your garden is brimming with zucchini, use it in this recipe along with—or instead of—the yellow squash. Refrigerate summer squash in a plastic bag for up to 5 days. Wash and trim ends before using.

SALADS & SIDES

avocado chicken salad

PREP/TOTAL TIME: 20 MIN.

1	medium ripe avocado, peeled and cubed
2	tablespoons lemon juice, *divided*
2	cups cubed cooked chicken
2	cups seedless red grapes, halved
1	medium tart apple, chopped
1	cup chopped celery
3/4	cup mayonnaise
1/2	cup chopped walnuts, toasted
1/2	teaspoon ground ginger

Lettuce leaves, optional

In a small bowl, toss avocado with 1 tablespoon lemon juice; set aside. In a large bowl, combine the chicken, grapes, apple, celery, mayonnaise, walnuts, ginger and remaining lemon juice. Stir in avocado. Serve on lettuce-lined plates if desired. **Yield:** 5 servings.

This is the first time I've ever shared this recipe, but it's one that my family and friends request for every outing we have!
I sometimes serve it in pita bread for a filling grab-and-go lunch.

KARLENE JOHNSON
MOORESVILLE
NORTH CAROLINA

tuna-stuffed tomatoes

PREP/TOTAL TIME: 10 MIN.

4	large tomatoes
1/2	cup mayonnaise
1/2	teaspoon celery salt
1/2	teaspoon dill weed
1/4	teaspoon pepper
2	cans (6 ounces *each*) tuna, drained and flaked
2	celery ribs, chopped
1/2	cup chopped cashews, optional

Cut a thin slice off the top of each tomato. Scoop out the pulp, leaving a 1/2-in. shell for each. Invert the tomatoes onto paper towels to drain.

In a bowl, combine the mayonnaise, celery salt, dill and pepper. Stir in the tuna, celery and cashews if desired. Spoon into tomato shells. **Yield:** 4 servings.

Fresh tomatoes are hollowed out, and then filled with a flavorful tuna salad mixture that gets crunch from celery and cashews.

TASTE OF HOME
TEST KITCHEN

 Timely Tuna Salad: Assemble the tuna salad in the morning or even the night before. When you get home, make and drain the tomato shells. Gather your other dinner items, then spoon the tuna salad into the tomato shells.

SALADS & SIDES

lemon angel hair

PREP/TOTAL TIME: 20 MIN.

8	ounces uncooked angel hair pasta
1/4	cup minced fresh parsley
3	teaspoons grated lemon peel
2	teaspoons minced garlic
6	tablespoons olive oil
3	tablespoons lemon juice
1/2	teaspoon salt
1/4	teaspoon pepper
1/3	cup grated Parmesan cheese

Cook pasta according to package directions. Meanwhile, in a large skillet, saute the parsley, lemon peel and garlic in oil until garlic is tender.

Drain pasta; add to the skillet. Sprinkle with lemon juice, salt and pepper; toss to coat. Top with Parmesan cheese. **Yield:** 4 servings.

Angel hair pasta gets loads of flavor from lemon and Parmesan cheese. A hint of garlic and flecks of fresh parsley add interest, too. This simple side goes well with chicken, fish, seafood or pork.

**MEG MONGELL
PLAINFIELD, INDIANA**

Lemon Lesson:
One lemon yields 2-3 tablespoons juice and about 1 tablespoon grated peel.

skillet lo mein

PREP/TOTAL TIME: 20 MIN.

4	ounces uncooked spaghetti, broken into thirds
1	tablespoon vegetable oil
1	package (9 ounces) frozen Szechuan stir-fry vegetables with sauce, thawed
1/3	cup julienned carrot
1/4	cup sliced celery
1/4	cup sliced onion
2	tablespoons soy sauce
1/8	teaspoon ground ginger

Cook the spaghetti according to directions. Meanwhile, in a skillet, heat oil over medium-high heat; stir in the stir-fry vegetables, contents of seasoning packet and remaining ingredients. Bring to a boil. Reduce heat; simmer, uncovered, for 3-4 minutes or until vegetables are crisp-tender. Drain spaghetti; stir into vegetables. **Yield:** 4 servings.

For a worthy side dish, offer up this tasty combination coated in a savory Szechuan sauce.

DEBBIE STADTLER
FREDERICKSBURG, VIRGINIA

sesame green bean salad

PREP/TOTAL TIME: 20 MIN.

1	pound fresh green beans, trimmed
1	tablespoon soy sauce
2	teaspoons canola oil
1	teaspoon sugar
1	teaspoon cider vinegar
1	teaspoon sesame oil
1/4	teaspoon salt
2	teaspoons sesame seeds, toasted

Place the beans in a large saucepan and cover with water. Bring to a boil. Cook, uncovered, for 8-10 minutes or until crisp-tender. Drain and rinse in cold water; pat dry. Place beans in a serving bowl.

In a small bowl, whisk the soy sauce, canola oil, sugar, vinegar, sesame oil and salt. Pour over beans and toss to coat. Sprinkle with sesame seeds; toss again. Serve at room temperature. **Yield:** 5 servings.

Someone asks for the recipe for this chilled salad every time I make it. It's a refreshing dish that's great for potlucks and other get-togethers.

TERRI MCKAY
NEW BERN, NORTH CAROLINA

SALADS & SIDES

 ## almond strawberry salad

PREP/TOTAL TIME: 10 MIN.

3	cups fresh baby spinach
1/2	cup sliced fresh strawberries
1/4	cup sliced honey-roasted almonds
1	tablespoon cider vinegar
1	tablespoon honey
1-1/2	teaspoons sugar

In a large bowl, combine the spinach, strawberries and almonds. In a jar with a tight-fitting lid, combine the vinegar, honey and sugar; shake well. Drizzle over salad and toss to coat. **Yield:** 4 servings.

Everyone loves this pretty salad that's topped with strawberries and sliced almonds. With just a few ingredients, it's loaded with flavor.

RENAE ROSSOW
UNION, KENTUCKY

broccoli with yellow pepper

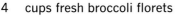

PREP/TOTAL TIME: 20 MIN.

4	cups fresh broccoli florets
4	teaspoons olive oil
1	medium sweet yellow pepper, cut into 2-inch thin strips
2	garlic cloves, minced
1	teaspoon minced fresh gingerroot

Salt and pepper to taste

In a wok or large skillet, stir-fry broccoli in oil until crisp-tender. Add the yellow pepper, garlic and ginger; stir-fry for 1-2 minutes or until heated through. Season with salt and pepper. **Yield:** 6 servings.

Including a yellow pepper adds both flavor and color to this broccoli side dish.

DOROTHY ELLIOTT
DEKALB, ILLINOIS

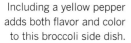

How Much Broccoli? One pound broccoli yields about 3-1/2 cups florets. So buy a little more than a pound for this recipe.

SALADS & SIDES

 warm dill potato salad

PREP/TOTAL TIME: 30 MIN.

1-1/2	pounds potatoes, peeled and cut into 1/2-inch cubes
1	tablespoon butter
1	tablespoon all-purpose flour
3/4	to 1 teaspoon salt
1/2	teaspoon dill seed
1/8	teaspoon pepper
1	cup milk
1/2	cup mayonnaise
2	tablespoons finely chopped onion
1/4	teaspoon paprika

Place potatoes in a large saucepan and cover with water. Bring to a boil. Reduce heat; cover and simmer for 8-10 minutes or until tender. Drain and set aside.

In a large skillet, melt butter; stir in the flour, salt, dill and pepper until blended. Gradually add milk. Bring to a boil; cook and stir for 2 minutes or until thickened and bubbly.

Remove from the heat. Stir in mayonnaise and onion. Add the potatoes; toss gently to coat. Sprinkle with paprika. Serve immediately. **Yield:** 5 servings.

Everyone who tries this warm potato salad is delighted. It's a nice change of pace from other varieties. A friend gave me the recipe a long time ago, and we've been enjoying it ever since.

BETTY CLAYCOMB
ALVERTON, PENNSYLVANIA

Selecting Potatoes: Any type of potatoes can be used in Warm Dill Potato Salad. Always select well-shaped, firm potatoes that are free from cuts, decay, blemishes or green discoloration. Avoid sprouted or shriveled potatoes.

sweet corn 'n' peppers

PREP/TOTAL TIME: 30 MIN.

1 medium sweet red pepper, julienned
1 medium green pepper, julienned
1 medium jalapeno pepper, seeded and julienned
1 medium sweet onion, cut into thin wedges
1/2 teaspoon salt
1/2 teaspoon pepper
1/8 teaspoon cayenne pepper
Dash paprika
6 large ears sweet corn, husks removed and halved

In a bowl, combine the peppers and onion. Combine the salt, pepper, cayenne and paprika; sprinkle half over the vegetables and set aside. Sprinkle remaining seasoning mixture over corn.

Place the corn on a vegetable grilling rack coated with cooking spray or in a perforated disposable aluminum pan.

Grill, covered, over medium heat for 10 minutes. Add reserved vegetables. Grill, covered, 5-10 minutes longer or until vegetables are tender, stirring occasionally and rotating corn. **Yield:** 6 servings.

EDITOR'S NOTE: When cutting hot peppers, disposable gloves are recommended. Avoid touching your face.

Peppers add punch to this mouthwatering grilled sweet corn. It's so pretty on the table.

GRACE CAMP
OWINGSVILLE, KENTUCKY

SALADS & SIDES

marinated vegetable salad

PREP: 20 MIN. + CHILLING

2	cups fresh broccoli florets
2	cups fresh cauliflowerets
1	medium cucumber, halved and thinly sliced
1	cup sliced fresh mushrooms
1	cup cherry tomatoes, halved
1/3	cup finely chopped red onion
1/2	cup Italian salad dressing

In a large bowl, combine the broccoli, cauliflower, cucumber, mushrooms, tomatoes and onion. Add dressing and toss to coat. Cover and refrigerate for 8 hours or overnight. **Yield:** 6 servings.

Toss some good-for-you veggies together with a coating of salad dressing, and you've got this ideal side dish in no time. Marinating the vegetables overnight gives them great flavor and texture.

**SARAH NEWMAN
BROOKLYN CENTER
MINNESOTA**

Easy Salad Dressing: For a simple Italian salad dressing with homemade taste, combine 1/3 cup sugar, 1 envelope Italian salad dressing mix, 3 minced garlic cloves, 3/4 cup cider vinegar and 3/4 cup water. Gradually whisk in 3/4 cup canola oil. Store in the refrigerator; stir before serving.

thai beef salad

PREP/TOTAL TIME: 20 MIN.

7	tablespoons olive oil, *divided*
2	tablespoons lime juice, *divided*
2	tablespoons chili sauce
1/2	teaspoon dried cilantro flakes
6	cups shredded napa *or* Chinese cabbage
2	cups shredded carrots
1	cup chopped seeded peeled cucumber
1-1/2	pounds boneless beef sirloin steak, cut into thin strips
2	teaspoons minced garlic
1	teaspoon ground coriander
1	teaspoon dried basil

In a jar with a tight-fitting lid, combine 6 tablespoons oil, 1 tablespoon lime juice, chili sauce and cilantro; shake well. In a large bowl, combine the cabbage, carrots and cucumber. Drizzle with dressing and toss to coat; arrange on four plates.

In a large skillet, cook the beef, garlic, coriander and basil in remaining oil for 5-6 minutes or until meat is no longer pink. Sprinkle with the remaining lime juice. Spoon the beef and pan juices over salad. **Yield:** 4 servings.

Napa cabbage, also known as Chinese cabbage, has white ribs and green leaves. It's commonly used in Asian cooking and can be found year-round in the produce section of your local grocery store.

TASTE OF HOME TEST KITCHEN

SALADS & SIDES

 baby carrots with almonds

PREP/TOTAL TIME: 10 MIN.

1   pound fresh baby carrots
2   tablespoons water
2   tablespoons slivered almonds, toasted
1   tablespoon sugar
1   tablespoon butter
1/8   teaspoon salt

Place carrots and water in a microwave-safe bowl. Cover and microwave on high for 4-6 minutes or until tender; drain. Stir in the remaining ingredients. **Yield:** 4 servings.

EDITOR'S NOTE: This recipe was tested in a 1,100-watt microwave.

These not-so-candied carrots are a treat for my diabetic husband, but they are actually something we all enjoy.

JANE KITTLE
COLUMBIA CROSS ROADS
PENNSYLVANIA

focaccia pork salad

PREP/TOTAL TIME: 25 MIN.

6	ounces focaccia bread, cubed
3/4	pound honey-mustard center cut pork loin fillet, cut into 1-inch pieces
2	teaspoons plus 1/4 cup olive oil, *divided*
4	cups torn romaine
1/2	cup crumbled blue cheese
2	tablespoons balsamic vinegar
1/2	teaspoon dried oregano

Place bread cubes on an ungreased baking sheet. Bake at 400° for 8-10 minutes or until golden brown.

Meanwhile, in a large skillet, brown pork in 2 teaspoons oil over medium heat for 5-6 minutes or until no longer pink.

In a large bowl, combine the romaine, blue cheese, bread cubes and pork. In a small bowl, whisk the vinegar, oregano and remaining oil. Drizzle over salad and toss to coat. Serve immediately. **Yield:** 6 servings.

Dinner's done in no time with this easy salad flavored with honey-mustard pork, blue cheese and a simple three-ingredient dressing.

**TASTE OF HOME
TEST KITCHEN**

 Pick a Pork Loin: Your grocer's meat department likely carries marinated pork loin fillets in a variety of flavors, including honey-mustard, lemon-garlic and teriyaki. Use whichever one you and your family prefer in this simple salad.

SALADS & SIDES

 ## green beans with red pepper

PREP/TOTAL TIME: 30 MIN.

1-1/2	pounds fresh green beans, trimmed
1/3	cup water
6	tablespoons butter
3/4	cup sliced sweet red pepper
1	tablespoon chopped shallot
Salt and pepper to taste	
1/3	cup sliced almonds, toasted

Place beans and water in a 2-qt. microwave-safe dish. Cover and microwave on high for 6-8 minutes or until crisp-tender.

Meanwhile, in a large skillet, melt butter; add red pepper and shallot. Cook, uncovered, over medium heat until red pepper is crisp-tender.

Drain beans; stir into red pepper mixture. Season with salt and pepper. Transfer to a serving platter; sprinkle with almonds. **Yield:** 5 servings.

EDITOR'S NOTE: This recipe was tested in a 1,100-watt microwave.

This is one of our favorite in-a-snap side dishes. It's also a beautiful addition to any holiday plate.

**TRACEY MEDEIROS
ATLANTA, GEORGIA**

Save Time Trimming:
To easily trim the ends of many green beans at one time, gather the beans in a bunch and line up the stem ends. Cut off the ends with a sharp knife. Repeat on the other side.

mashed potatoes with corn and cheese

PREP/TOTAL TIME: 25 MIN.

4	cups cubed peeled potatoes
1-1/2	cups water
4	to 6 tablespoons milk
3	tablespoons butter, softened
1/2	teaspoon salt
1/4	teaspoon pepper
1	cup frozen corn, thawed and warmed
1-1/2	cups (6 ounces) shredded Colby-Monterey Jack cheese

Place potatoes and water in a microwave-safe dish. Cover and microwave on high for 12-14 minutes or until tender; drain.

Place potatoes in a bowl; mash with milk, butter, salt and pepper. Stir in corn and cheese. **Yield:** 6 servings.

EDITOR'S NOTE: This recipe was tested in a 1,100-watt microwave.

Who knew that already delicious mashed potatoes could get any better? Cheese and corn add a boost of flavor and color.

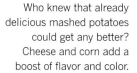

TASTE OF HOME
TEST KITCHEN

SALADS & SIDES

orange fruit slaw

PREP/TOTAL TIME: 20 MIN.

3	cups shredded cabbage
1	medium navel orange, peeled and sectioned
1	cup seedless red grapes, halved
1	medium apple, chopped
1/2	cup finely chopped celery
1	carton (6 ounces) orange yogurt
1/4	teaspoon salt
1/8	teaspoon pepper
1/4	cup slivered almonds, toasted

In a large bowl, combine the cabbage, orange, grapes, apple and celery. Stir in the yogurt, salt and pepper; toss until well coated. Cover and refrigerate until serving. Sprinkle with almonds just before serving. **Yield:** 6 servings.

I love this fruity coleslaw. My neighbor shared it with our women's church group a few years ago, and it's been a favorite in my recipe box ever since.

CYNTHIA FRANCE
MURRAY, UTAH

Toasting Nuts: To toast nuts on the stovetop, heat a dry skillet until hot. Pour in nuts and spread in a single layer. Stir frequently for 3-5 minutes. Watch carefully to avoid burning.

roasted vegetables with orzo

PREP/TOTAL TIME: 30 MIN.

1	cup uncooked orzo pasta
1	cup cherry tomatoes
1/2	cup *each* chopped green and sweet red pepper
1/4	cup chopped onion
2	tablespoons olive oil
1-3/4	teaspoons minced garlic
1/2	teaspoon salt
1/4	to 1/2 teaspoon pepper

Cook orzo according to package directions. Meanwhile, in an ungreased 2-qt. baking dish, combine the remaining ingredients.

Bake, uncovered, at 450° for 15-20 minutes or until the vegetables are tender, stirring occasionally. Drain orzo; stir into vegetable mixture. **Yield:** 6 servings.

A little peppery heat warms up this tasty and versatile veggie-and-orzo side dish. I often substitute a variety of seasonal vegetables, and it's always delicious.

SAM STUSEK
ANNAPOLIS, MARYLAND

parmesan couscous

PREP/TOTAL TIME: 10 MIN.

1	cup water
1	tablespoon butter
3/4	cup uncooked couscous
1/4	cup grated Parmesan cheese
2	tablespoons chopped green onion
1	tablespoon diced pimientos
1	teaspoon minced garlic
1/4	teaspoon coarsely ground pepper
1/8	teaspoon salt

In a small saucepan, bring water and butter to a boil. Stir in couscous. Cover and remove from the heat; let stand for 5 minutes. Fluff with a fork. Stir in the remaining ingredients. **Yield:** 4 servings.

To accompany any main dish, whip this up on the stovetop in just 10 minutes.

TASTE OF HOME
TEST KITCHEN

festive corn 'n' broccoli

PREP/TOTAL TIME: 15 MIN.

1	package (16 ounces) frozen chopped broccoli, thawed
1	can (7 ounces) Mexicorn, drained
1/4	cup butter, cubed
1	teaspoon dried basil
1/2	teaspoon salt
1/8	teaspoon garlic powder
1/8	teaspoon pepper

In a large skillet, combine the broccoli, corn and butter; cook over medium heat until butter is melted. Stir in the basil, salt, garlic powder and pepper. Cover and cook for 8-10 minutes or until the vegetables are tender, stirring occasionally. **Yield:** 5 servings.

Jazz up broccoli and corn with simple seasonings. I serve this side dish alongside any meaty entree.

LUCILE THROGMORTON
CLOVIS, NEW MEXICO

SALADS & SIDES

white 'n' sweet mashed potatoes

PREP/TOTAL TIME: 30 MIN.

1-1/2	pounds russet potatoes (about 4 medium), peeled and cubed
1-1/2	pounds sweet potatoes (about 4 medium), peeled and cubed
1	cup milk, warmed
1/4	cup butter, cubed
1	teaspoon salt
1/2	teaspoon ground cinnamon
1/4	teaspoon ground nutmeg

Place russet potatoes and sweet potatoes in a large saucepan and cover with water. Bring to a boil. Reduce heat; cover and simmer for 15-20 minutes or until tender. Drain.

In a large bowl, mash the potatoes with the milk, butter, salt, cinnamon and nutmeg until potatoes reach desired consistency. **Yield:** 8 servings.

Sweet potatoes are a staple of Southern cooking here in North Carolina. Combined with russet potatoes, this recipe makes simple mashed potatoes a very special treat.

**GAIL DREWS
FLAT ROCK
NORTH CAROLINA**

Sweet Potatoes or Yams?
Sweet potatoes and yams are similar in many ways, so they're often confused with one another. Two varieties of sweet potatoes are readily available. One has a pale skin with a light yellow flesh and a dry, mealy texture. The other—commonly known as a yam—has dark skin with a dark orange flesh that cooks to a moist texture. True yams, though, are not readily available in this country. Sweet potatoes and yams are interchangeable in most recipes.

herbed potatoes and veggies

PREP/TOTAL TIME: 25 MIN.

30

4	medium baking potatoes
1-1/2	cups diced zucchini
3	tablespoons olive oil
2	tablespoons plus 1 teaspoon savory herb with garlic soup mix
1/4	teaspoon pepper
10	cherry tomatoes, halved

Scrub and pierce potatoes; place on a microwave-safe plate. Cover and microwave on high for 5-6 minutes on each side or until tender. When potatoes are cool enough to handle, cut into cubes.

In a large skillet, saute potatoes and zucchini in oil for 5 minutes or until vegetables are tender. Sprinkle with soup mix and pepper. Cook until heated through, stirring occasionally. Add tomatoes; cook 1 minute longer. **Yield:** 6 servings.

EDITOR'S NOTE: This recipe was tested in a 1,100-watt microwave.

I came up with this family favorite when I needed to use up leftover baked potatoes and extra produce from our garden. It's a great-tasting side dish. My husband requests it all the time and brags about it to company.

JENELLE PARKS
HAYFIELD, MINNESOTA

SALADS & SIDES

stuffed iceberg wedges

PREP: 20 MIN. + CHILLING

1	medium head iceberg lettuce
1/3	cup mayonnaise
1/4	teaspoon curry powder
1	cup (4 ounces) shredded cheddar cheese
1/2	cup coarsely chopped fully cooked ham
1/2	cup chopped celery
1/4	cup minced fresh parsley
1	jar (2 ounces) diced pimientos, drained

Salad dressing of your choice

Remove core from the head of lettuce. Carefully hollow out lettuce, leaving a 3/4-in. shell (save removed lettuce for another use).

In a small bowl, combine the mayonnaise and curry powder. Add the cheese, ham, celery, parsley and pimientos; mix well. Spoon into lettuce shell. Tightly wrap in plastic wrap; refrigerate for at least 3 hours. Cut into wedges. Serve with the salad dressing. **Yield:** 4-6 servings.

Perfectly seasoned ham salad is tucked inside crisp iceberg lettuce for a refreshing entree.

ROSEMARIE SURWILLO
LAKE ST. LOUIS, MISSOURI

basil baked tomatoes

PREP/TOTAL TIME: 25 MIN.

1	garlic clove, minced
1	tablespoon olive oil
1/2	cup soft bread crumbs
2	large tomatoes
4	fresh basil leaves, chopped
1/8	teaspoon coarsely ground pepper

In a small skillet, saute the garlic in oil for 1 minute. Add bread crumbs; cook and stir until lightly browned. Remove from the heat.

Cut tomatoes in half widthwise. Place cut side up in an 8-in. square baking dish. Sprinkle with basil and pepper; top with bread crumb mixture. Bake at 325° for 15-20 minutes or until the tomatoes are slightly softened. **Yield:** 4 servings.

This recipe has been in our family for many years. My mother brought it with her when she came to the United States from Italy. When fresh tomatoes are plentiful, this is a great way to serve them.

MARY DETZI
WIND GAP, PENNSYLVANIA

 Best Baked Tomatoes: Firm tomatoes that are not overripe will best hold their shape while baking. For added stability, place the stuffed tomatoes in a muffin tin and bake as directed.

SALADS & SIDES

 ## sidesaddle pork 'n' beans

PREP/TOTAL TIME: 20 MIN.

1/2	pound bulk pork sausage
1/3	cup chopped onion
1	can (15-3/4 ounces) pork and beans
1/4	cup barbecue sauce
3	tablespoons honey
2	tablespoons ketchup
1/8	teaspoon salt, optional
1/8	teaspoon dried rosemary, crushed
1/8	teaspoon dried thyme
1/8	teaspoon Cajun seasoning

In a large skillet, cook the sausage and onion over medium heat until meat is no longer pink; drain. Stir in the beans, barbecue sauce, honey, ketchup and seasonings. Bring to a boil. Reduce heat; simmer, uncovered, for 5-8 minutes or until slightly thickened. **Yield:** 8 servings.

Sweet pork 'n' beans makes a hearty, lickety-split side dish and brings real barbecue flavor to the table any time of year. My family loves it.

**JANET DOHERTY
BELPRE, OHIO**

Down-Home Dinner:
Pork and beans calls for a kid-friendly dinner! Separate refrigerated corn bread twists into 8 strips. Wrap one strip around a hot dog. Brush with melted butter. Place on a lightly greased baking sheet. Bake at 375° for 11-13 minutes or until golden brown.

instant fried rice

PREP/TOTAL TIME: 20 MIN.

1	envelope fried rice seasoning
2	tablespoons water
2	green onions, chopped
2	tablespoons canola oil
1	egg, lightly beaten
3	cups cold cooked instant rice
1/2	cup peas

In a small bowl, combine seasoning mix and water; set aside. In a large skillet or wok, stir-fry onions in oil for 2-3 minutes. Add egg; stir until scrambled.

Add rice and peas; stir-fry until heated through. Stir in seasoning mixture; stir-fry 3-4 minutes longer or until heated through. **Yield:** 4 servings.

Instant rice and a seasoning pack cut prep time for this fast, fuss-free and delicious fried-rice.

AMY CORLEW-SHERLOCK
LAPEER, MICHIGAN

almond spinach salad

PREP/TOTAL TIME: 15 MIN.

1	package (10 ounces) fresh spinach, torn
1	medium tomato, sliced
1/2	cup thinly sliced red onion
1/2	medium ripe avocado, peeled and sliced
1/4	cup sliced almonds, toasted
1/3	to 1/2 cup red wine vinaigrette

In a large salad bowl, combine the spinach, tomato, onion, avocado and almonds. Drizzle with vinaigrette and toss to coat. Serve immediately. **Yield:** 4 servings.

This easy tossed salad is colorful, fresh and crunchy.

KARENA LEE
SUNLAND, CALIFORNIA

ranch pasta salad

PREP/TOTAL TIME: 25 MIN.

3	cups uncooked tricolor spiral pasta
1	cup chopped fresh broccoli florets
3/4	cup chopped seeded peeled cucumber
1/2	cup seeded chopped tomato
1	bottle (8 ounces) ranch salad dressing
1/2	cup shredded Parmesan cheese

Cook pasta according to package directions; drain and rinse in cold water. In a large bowl, combine the pasta, broccoli, cucumber and tomato. Drizzle with salad dressing; toss to coat. Sprinkle with the Parmesan cheese. **Yield:** 8 servings.

I've made this salad for years—it's a recipe from a high school friend's mom. Any time I serve a sandwich meal like hamburgers, hot dogs or sloppy joes, I have this flavorful salad alongside.

KRISTA COLLINS
CONCORD, NORTH CAROLINA

SALADS & SIDES

 pineapple coleslaw

PREP/TOTAL TIME: 10 MIN.

2	cups coleslaw mix
1	cup unsweetened crushed pineapple, drained
1/3	cup shredded carrot
3	medium radishes, shredded
1/4	teaspoon celery seed
1/3	cup mayonnaise

In a large bowl, combine the first five ingredients. Add mayonnaise and toss to coat. Cover and refrigerate until serving. **Yield:** 4 servings.

The cool, refreshing crunch of this coleslaw makes it a welcome addition to many meals. Pineapple lends a sweet tang.

SHIRLEY GLAAB
HATTIESBURG, MISSISSIPPI

Lively Leftovers: A 10-ounce bag of ready-to-use shredded carrots equals about 3-1/2 cups. Use 1/3 cup to make Pineapple Coleslaw now. Refrigerate the unused portion in the original bag and use the remaining to make Sunny Carrot Salad, page 189, in a few days.

basil walnut fettuccine

PREP/TOTAL TIME: 20 MIN.

1	package (12 ounces) fettuccine
1	teaspoon minced garlic
6	tablespoons butter, *divided*
1/4	cup finely chopped walnuts, toasted
1	tablespoon minced fresh basil *or* 1 teaspoon dried basil
1/4	teaspoon salt
1/8	teaspoon pepper

Cook fettuccine according to package directions. In a large skillet, saute garlic in 1 tablespoon butter for 1 minute or until crisp-tender. Add the walnuts, basil, salt, pepper and the remaining butter; cook and stir for 2 minutes or until heated through. Drain fettuccine; add to skillet and toss to coat. **Yield:** 6 servings.

Buttery fettuccine is studded with toasted nuts and lightly flavored with garlic and fresh basil. It goes well with a variety of entrees.

TASTE OF HOME
TEST KITCHEN

SALADS & SIDES

black bean asparagus salad

PREP/TOTAL TIME: 15 MIN.

1 pound fresh asparagus, trimmed and cut into 1-inch pieces
1 can (15 ounces) black beans, rinsed and drained
1 medium sweet red pepper, cut into 1/2-inch pieces
1 tablespoon finely chopped onion
3 tablespoons olive oil
2 tablespoons cider vinegar
1 tablespoon minced fresh cilantro
1 garlic clove, minced
1/2 teaspoon salt
1/2 teaspoon ground cumin
Dash pepper

Place 1/2 in. of water in a large saucepan; add asparagus. Bring to a boil. Reduce heat; cover and simmer for 4-5 minutes or until crisp-tender. Drain.

In a bowl, combine the asparagus, beans, red pepper and onion. In a small bowl, whisk the oil, vinegar, cilantro, garlic, salt, cumin and pepper. Pour over vegetables and toss to coat. Cover and refrigerate for at least 2 hours before serving. **Yield:** 8 servings.

Do you like asparagus but want something beyond plain, steamed asparagus? Try this refreshing new salad idea. The black beans, red pepper, cilantro and cumin give it a Southwest twist.

LAURIE JACKSON
FALCON, COLORADO

Blend the Flavors:
To give Black Bean Asparagus Salad even more robust flavor, prepare the night before, cover and chill. Top with additional fresh cilantro just before serving.

feta-olive romaine salad

PREP/TOTAL TIME: 15 MIN.

6	cups torn romaine
2/3	cup diced sweet red pepper
1/3	cup diced green pepper
3	tablespoons chopped ripe olives
1/4	cup olive oil
1/4	cup balsamic vinegar
1/3	cup tomato and basil feta cheese, crumbled

In a salad bowl, toss the romaine, peppers and olives. In a jar with a tight-fitting lid, combine oil and vinegar; shake well. Drizzle over salad and toss to coat. Sprinkle with feta cheese. **Yield:** 4-6 servings.

This easy Greek salad with a homemade dressing is loaded with flavor.

ANITA KEPPINGER
PHILOMATH, OREGON

nectarine and beet salad

PREP/TOTAL TIME: 10 MIN.

2	packages (5 ounces *each*) spring mix salad greens
2	cups sliced fresh nectarines
1	can (13-1/4 ounces) sliced beets, drained
1/2	cup balsamic vinaigrette
1/2	cup crumbled feta cheese

In a large salad bowl, combine the greens, nectarines and beets. Drizzle with dressing and toss gently to coat. Sprinkle with cheese. **Yield:** 8 servings.

The combination of ingredients in this colorful salad may seem unlikely, but it's delicious!

NICOLE WERNER
CLEVELAND HEIGHTS, OHIO

skillet sausage stuffing

PREP/TOTAL TIME: 25 MIN.

1	pound bulk pork sausage
1-1/4	cups chopped celery
1/2	cup chopped onion
1/2	cup sliced fresh mushrooms
1-1/2	teaspoons minced garlic
1-1/2	cups chicken broth
1	teaspoon rubbed sage
1	package (6 ounces) stuffing mix

In a large skillet, cook the sausage, celery, onion, mushrooms and garlic over medium heat until meat is no longer pink; drain. Stir in broth and sage. Bring to a boil. Stir in the stuffing mix. Cover and remove from the heat; let stand for 5 minutes. Fluff with a fork. **Yield:** 8 servings.

I dressed up a package of stuffing mix with pork sausage, mushrooms, celery and onion. It impressed my in-laws at a family gathering and has since become a popular side dish with my husband and children.

JENNIFER LYNN CULLEN
TAYLOR, MICHIGAN

SALADS & SIDES

cherry tomato corn salad

PREP/TOTAL TIME: 15 MIN.

1/4	cup minced fresh basil
3	tablespoons olive oil
2	teaspoons lime juice
1	teaspoon sugar
1/2	teaspoon salt
1/4	teaspoon pepper
2	cups frozen corn, thawed
2	cups cherry tomatoes, halved
1	cup chopped seeded peeled cucumber

In a jar with a tight-fitting lid, combine the basil, oil, lime juice, sugar, salt and pepper; shake well.

In a large bowl, combine the corn, tomatoes and cucumber. Drizzle with the dressing; toss to coat. Refrigerate until ready to serve. **Yield:** 6 servings.

In the summer, use fresh sweet corn off the cob. Saute the corn for 5 minutes in a skillet before adding it to the salad.

TASTE OF HOME TEST KITCHEN

Seeding a Cucumber: To easily seed a cucumber, cut a peeled cucumber in half lengthwise. With a teaspoon, run the tip under the seeds to loosen and remove.

sunny carrot salad

PREP/TOTAL TIME: 10 MIN.

3	cups shredded carrots
2	cups unsweetened crushed pineapple, drained
1/2	cup golden raisins
1/3	cup mayonnaise
1/2	cup sliced almonds
1/3	cup unsalted sunflower kernels

In a large serving bowl, combine the carrots, pineapple and raisins. Stir in mayonnaise. Cover and refrigerate until serving. Just before serving, add almonds and sunflower kernels; toss to coat. **Yield:** 5 servings.

Almonds and sunflower kernels give a pleasing crunch to this speedy variation on traditional carrot-raisin salad.

**BARB HUNTER
PONDER, TEXAS**

SALADS & SIDES

black bean shrimp salad

PREP: 15 MIN. + CHILLING

1	pound cooked medium shrimp, peeled and deveined
1	can (15 ounces) black beans, rinsed and drained
1	small green pepper, julienned
1	small onion, thinly sliced
1/2	cup chopped celery
2/3	cup picante sauce
2	tablespoons minced fresh cilantro
2	tablespoons lime juice
2	tablespoons olive oil
2	tablespoons honey
1/2	teaspoon salt
1/8	teaspoon grated lime peel, optional
6	lettuce leaves
1	cup halved cherry tomatoes

In a large bowl, combine the first five ingredients.

In a small bowl, whisk the picante sauce, cilantro, lime juice, oil, honey, salt and lime peel if desired. Pour over shrimp mixture and toss to coat. Cover and refrigerate for at least 2 hours.

Using a slotted spoon, spoon onto a lettuce-lined serving platter or salad plates. Garnish with tomatoes. **Yield:** 6 servings.

I lived in Venezuela for several years, so this Caribbean-style salad is a favorite of mine. I came across the recipe about 10 years ago and changed it to suit my taste.

ROSEMARIE FORCUM
HEATHSVILLE, VIRGINIA

zucchini apple salad

PREP/TOTAL TIME: 10 MIN.

2	medium red apples, chopped
2	small zucchini, chopped
1/2	cup coarsely chopped walnuts
2/3	cup Italian salad dressing

In a serving bowl, toss the apples, zucchini, walnuts and salad dressing. **Yield:** 6 servings.

You'll want to serve this salad in a glass bowl because it's so colorful. Everyone will enjoy its fresh-tasting crunch, and you'll like how quickly it goes together!

LOIS FRAZEE
FERNLEY, NEVADA

 Chopping Nuts: Before chopping nuts in a food processor, dust them with flour. This keeps the nuts from sticking to the blade.

SALADS & SIDES

fiesta side salad

PREP: 30 MIN. + CHILLING

2/3	cup uncooked long grain rice
2	cups frozen corn, thawed
1	can (15 ounces) black beans, rinsed and drained
6	green onions, sliced
1/4	cup pickled jalapeno slices, chopped
1/4	cup canola oil
2	tablespoons cider vinegar
1	tablespoon lime juice
1	teaspoon chili powder
1	teaspoon molasses
1/2	teaspoon salt
1/2	teaspoon cumin seeds, toasted and ground

Cook rice according to package directions. Meanwhile, in a large bowl, combine the corn, beans, onions and jalapenos. In a jar with a tight-fitting lid, combine the remaining ingredients; shake well.

Stir rice into corn mixture. Add dressing and toss to coat. Cover and refrigerate for at least 2 hours. **Yield:** 8 servings.

Perfect for a buffet, picnic or potluck, this colorful side can be served at room temperature. You'll want to make extra because the flavors only get better the second day.

MICHELLE CHICOINE
APO, AE

Cumin Seeds Make It Special:
Toasting whole cumin seeds and then grinding them adds extra flavor to this salad. If you don't have whole cumin seeds, substitute 1/4 teaspoon of ground cumin—don't toast.

chocolate silk pie, pg. 223

DESSERTS

grasshopper pie

PREP: 15 MIN. + CHILLING

1-1/2	cups cold milk
1	package (3.9 ounces) instant chocolate pudding mix
2-3/4	cups whipped topping, *divided*
1	package (4.67 ounces) mint Andes candies, chopped, *divided*
1	chocolate crumb crust (9 inches)
1/4	teaspoon mint extract
2	drops green food coloring, optional

In a small bowl, whisk milk and pudding mix for 2 minutes. Let stand for 2 minutes or until soft-set. Fold in 3/4 cup whipped topping. Fold in 3/4 cup candies. Spoon into the crust.

In another bowl, combine the extract and remaining whipped topping; add food coloring if desired. Spread over pudding layer; sprinkle with remaining candies. Cover and refrigerate for 4 hours or until set. **Yield:** 8 servings.

This pie has become a Christmas classic in our family. Although now, I make it throughout the year!

MELISSA SOKASITS
ARRENVILLE, ILLINOIS

black forest sundaes

PREP/TOTAL TIME: 5 MIN.

1/2	cup crushed cream-filled chocolate sandwich cookies
4	scoops vanilla ice cream
1	can (21 ounces) cherry pie filling

Whipped cream in a can
Chopped walnuts

Divide cookie crumbs among four dessert dishes; top each with ice cream and pie filling. Garnish with whipped cream and walnuts. Freeze until serving. **Yield:** 4 servings.

This dessert makes a sweet ending. Best of all, the sundaes take just five minutes to prepare. My husband and grandchildren love them.

RUTH LEE
TROY, ONTARIO

Try This Taste Twist: Vary the flavor of these sundaes by replacing cream-filled vanilla sandwich cookies for the chocolate cookies and apple pie filling for the cherry filling.

DESSERTS

chocolate-dipped strawberries
PREP/TOTAL TIME: 20 MIN.

1 pint large strawberries
4 ounces semisweet chocolate, chopped
1 tablespoon plus 1/2 teaspoon shortening, *divided*
1 ounce white baking chocolate
4 drops food coloring, optional

Wash strawberries and gently pat with paper towels until completely dry. In a microwave-safe bowl, melt semisweet chocolate and 1 tablespoon shortening at 50% power; stir until smooth. Dip strawberries and place on a waxed paper-lined baking sheet. Freeze strawberries for 5 minutes.

Meanwhile, microwave the white chocolate and remaining shortening at 30% power until melted; stir until smooth. Stir in the food coloring if desired. Drizzle over the strawberries. Refrigerate until serving. **Yield:** about 9 strawberries.

Plump berries from our strawberry patch turned into a real treat when I dipped them in chocolate! I like to make these before dinner and put them in the fridge, so they're ready when we're finished eating.
**VALERIE GEE
DEPEW, NEW YORK**

Making Dipped Strawberries:
Ideally, strawberries for dipping should be chilled and be at least 1-1/2 inches in diameter.

frosty key lime pie

PREP: 20 MIN. + FREEZING

1   can (14 ounces) sweetened condensed milk

6   tablespoons key lime juice

2   cups heavy whipping cream, whipped, *divided*

1   graham cracker crust (9 inches)

In a large bowl, combine milk and lime juice. Refrigerate 1/4 cup whipped cream for garnish. Fold a fourth of the remaining whipped cream into lime mixture; fold in remaining whipped cream. Spoon into crust. Cover and freeze overnight.

Remove from the freezer 10-15 minutes before serving. Garnish with the reserved whipped cream. **Yield:** 6-8 servings.

Credit whipped cream for the fluffy-smooth texture and luscious flavor of this frozen refresher.

LISA FELD
GRAFTON, WISCONSIN

DESSERTS

dark chocolate fondue

PREP/TOTAL TIME: 20 MIN.

2   tablespoons all-purpose flour
1-1/2   cups 2% milk
2   dark chocolate candy bars
    (1.55 ounces *each*), chopped
3   squares (1 ounce *each*) milk
    chocolate, chopped
2   tablespoons light corn syrup
Cubed angel food cake and assorted
    fresh fruit

In a small saucepan, combine the flour and milk until smooth. Bring to a boil over medium-high heat; cook and stir for 1 minute or until thickened. Reduce the heat to low. Stir in the chocolate and corn syrup. Cook and stir until melted.

Transfer to a small fondue pot and keep warm. Serve with cake cubes and fruit. **Yield: 2 cups.**

Savor all the decadence without a lick of guilt! We kept all the velvety, melt-in-your-mouth texture of fudgy fondue in this lusciously lighter version.

**TASTE OF HOME
TEST KITCHEN**

luscious fudgy brownies

PREP: 15 MIN. BAKE: 20 MIN. + COOLING

1	cup sugar
3	tablespoons butter, melted
3	tablespoons vanilla yogurt
1	teaspoon vanilla extract
1	egg, lightly beaten
3/4	cup all-purpose flour
1/3	cup baking cocoa
1/8	teaspoon salt

In a small bowl, combine the sugar, butter, yogurt and vanilla. Stir in egg until blended. Combine the flour, cocoa and salt; stir into sugar mixture. Transfer to an 8-in. square baking dish coated with cooking spray.

Bake at 350° for 20-25 minutes or until a toothpick inserted near the center comes out clean and brownies begin to pull away from sides of pan. Cool on a wire rack. Cut into eight pieces, then cut each diagonally in half. **Yield:** 16 brownies.

This is a favorite after-dinner treat. I'm always very careful not to overbake these brownies because I love the ooey-gooey middle.

KRISTA FRANK
RHODODENDRON, OREGON

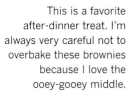

Dress Up Basic Brownies: When you remove the brownies from the oven, evenly sprinkle with miniature chocolate chips and miniature marshmallows. Put the brownies back in the oven until the marshmallows begin to soften.

DESSERTS

strawberry pie

PREP: 20 MIN. + COOLING BAKE: 10 MIN. + CHILLING

1	unbaked pastry shell (9 inches)
3/4	cup sugar
2	tablespoons cornstarch
1	cup water
1	package (3 ounces) strawberry gelatin
4	cups sliced fresh strawberries

Fresh mint, optional

Line unpricked pastry shell with a double thickness of heavy-duty foil. Bake at 450° for 8 minutes. Remove foil; bake 5 minutes longer. Cool on a wire rack.

In a saucepan, combine the sugar, cornstarch and water until smooth. Bring to a boil; cook and stir for 2 minutes or until thickened. Remove from the heat; stir in gelatin until dissolved. Refrigerate for 15-20 minutes or until slightly cooled.

Meanwhile, arrange strawberries in the crust. Pour gelatin mixture over berries. Refrigerate until set. Garnish with mint if desired. **Yield:** 6-8 servings.

I often use whole fresh strawberries and arrange them pointed side up in the pastry shell for a different presentation. It also is a time-saver because I don't have to slice the berries.

SUE JURACK
MEQUON, WISCONSIN

Stop Soggy Pie Crusts:
Pie crusts can often become soggy, especially when filled with fruit. To keep a crust crisp, brush the bottom and sides of the baked crust with a beaten egg after removing it from the oven. Return to the oven for a few minutes to set the glaze. Let cool and then fill as directed.

grilled cake and fruit

PREP/TOTAL TIME: 30 MIN.

4	slices angel food cake (1 inch thick)
1	square (1 ounce) bittersweet chocolate
1	medium firm banana, cut into fourths
8	pineapple chunks
1	tablespoon lemon juice
1/4	cup sugar
1/4	teaspoon ground cinnamon
2	medium kiwifruit, peeled and diced
8	fresh strawberries, sliced

Cut a pocket in each slice of cake by cutting from one long side to within 1/2 in. of the opposite side. Insert a chocolate piece into each opening; set aside.

In a small bowl, toss the banana, pineapple and lemon juice; drain. In a large resealable plastic bag, combine sugar and cinnamon. Add banana and pineapple; toss to coat. Thread onto four 4-in. metal or soaked wooden skewers.

Coat grill rack with cooking spray before starting the grill. Grill fruit over medium heat for 2-3 minutes on each side or until heated through.

Grill cake for 30-60 seconds on each side or until chocolate is melted. Combine kiwi, strawberries and grilled fruit; serve with the cake. **Yield:** 4 servings.

Grilled angel food cake slices are crisp outside and tender inside and complement melted chocolate and fresh fruit.
TERRI TRUDEAU
SAN GABRIEL, CALIFORNIA

DESSERTS

glazed apricot sorbet

PREP: 10 MIN. + FREEZING

1	can (20 ounces) apricot halves, drained
1	jar (10 ounces) apricot preserves
1-1/2	teaspoons grated orange peel
2	tablespoons lemon juice
5	tablespoons heavy whipping cream

In a food processor, combine the apricots, preserves, orange peel and lemon juice; cover and process until smooth. Pour into a freezer container; cover and freeze for at least 3 hours. The sorbet may be frozen for up to 3 months.

Remove from the freezer at least 15 minutes before serving. Scoop into dessert dishes; drizzle with cream. **Yield:** 5 servings.

This fruity dessert is refreshingly cool and light with a hint of richness. It's just right for a company meal or a pleasant afternoon treat. I like to serve it in sherbet glasses with mint sprigs for an elegant look.

NINA ROHLFS
UNADILLA, NEBRASKA

frosty pumpkinettes

PREP: 15 MIN. + FREEZING

1/4	cup canned pumpkin
2	tablespoons sugar
1-1/2	teaspoons molasses
1/8	teaspoon salt
1/8	teaspoon ground cinnamon
1/8	teaspoon ground ginger
3/4	cup vanilla ice cream, softened
4	individual graham cracker tart shells
1	tablespoon chopped pecans

In a small bowl, combine the pumpkin, sugar, molasses, salt, cinnamon and ginger; mix well. Fold in ice cream until smooth.

Spoon mixture into the tart shells; sprinkle with the pecans. Freeze for 1 hour or until serving. Remove from the freezer 10 minutes before serving. **Yield:** 4 tarts.

I've used this recipe since the early '50s when I picked it up at a seminar. I often prepare them as special treats for Halloween.

ELLA WEST
RICHMOND, VIRGINIA

 Fun Fillings for Graham Cracker Shells: Individual graham cracker tart shells are a simple way to dress up ordinary dessert. In addition to making Frosty Pumpkinettes, give these ideas a try:

Spoon cherry or apple pie filling into the shells; top with canned whipped cream. Or scoop out your family's favorite ice cream and place inside the graham cracker shells. Drizzle with chocolate, caramel or butterscotch ice cream topping. For a healthier option, fill the shells with cut-up fresh fruit.

peanut butter delights

PREP/TOTAL TIME: 30 MIN.

1	package (16 ounces) refrigerated ready-to-bake peanut butter cookies with candy pieces
2	tablespoons creamy peanut butter
3	ounces milk chocolate candy coating, melted

Bake cookies according to package directions. Cool on wire racks. Spread 12 cookies with 1/2 teaspoon peanut butter each; spoon melted chocolate over peanut butter. Let stand for 5 minutes or until set. Save remaining cookies for another use. **Yield:** 1 dozen.

With refrigerated cookie dough, these tasty cookies couldn't be quicker or easier. Everyone loves them—young or old.

JANICE RASMUSSEN
ATLANTIC, IOWA

DESERTS

cinnamon peach enchiladas

PREP/TOTAL TIME: 15 MIN.

4	cups sliced peeled fresh peaches
1/3	cup sugar
1	teaspoon ground cinnamon
4	flour tortillas (8 inches)

Butter-flavored cooking spray

In a large bowl, combine the peaches, sugar and cinnamon; let stand for 5 minutes. Spritz tortillas with butter-flavored spray.

In a nonstick skillet, cook tortillas over medium heat until warmed and lightly browned on both sides. Fill each with about 3/4 cup peaches and roll up. Cut in half to serve. **Yield:** 8 servings.

These sweet enchiladas are a pleasant change from traditional peach pie—and a whole lot easier. Simply fill warmed tortillas with a cinnamon-peach mixture, then wait for the compliments.

**IRENE GLEMBOTSKAYA
BROOKLYN, NEW YORK**

A Fast Way to Peel Peaches:
To easily peel peaches, first place them in a large pot of boiling water for 10-20 seconds or until the skins split. Remove with a slotted spoon. Immediately place in an ice water bath. Use a paring knife to peel. If stubborn areas of skin won't peel off, just return the fruit to the boiling water for a few more seconds.

cream cheese dessert wedges

PREP: 15 MIN. BAKE: 20 MIN. + COOLING

1	tube (7-1/2 ounces) refrigerated buttermilk biscuits
1	package (8 ounces) cream cheese, softened
1/2	cup sugar
1	egg
1	tablespoon all-purpose flour

TOPPING:

1	tablespoon sugar
1/2	teaspoon ground cinnamon

Separate biscuits into 10 pieces; place in an ungreased 9-in. round baking dish. Press onto the bottom and 1 in. up the sides, pinching edges together to seal. Bake at 350° for 5-7 minutes or until slightly puffed.

Meanwhile, in a small bowl, beat the cream cheese, sugar, egg and flour until smooth; pour over the crust. Combine the topping ingredients; sprinkle over the filling. Bake for 15-20 minutes or until filling is set and crust is golden brown.

Cool on a wire rack for at least 30 minutes before cutting. Serve warm or chilled. Refrigerate leftovers. **Yield:** 8-10 servings.

Refrigerated buttermilk biscuits create the tender crust for these pretty slices sprinkled with cinnamon and sugar. They can be served warm or chilled, and they're extra special with fresh fruit.

**BETTY CLAYCOMB
ALVERTON, PENNSYLVANIA**

DESSERTS

butterscotch angel cake

PREP/TOTAL TIME: 25 MIN.

8	slices angel food cake
3/4	cup butter, melted, *divided*
1	cup packed brown sugar, *divided*
8	scoops butter brickle *or* butter pecan ice cream

Butterscotch ice cream topping

Place cake slices on a greased baking sheet. Brush with 6 tablespoons butter; press 1 tablespoon brown sugar onto each slice. Broil 5-6 in. from the heat for 1-2 minutes or until bubbly.

Turn slices over; brush with remaining butter and sprinkle with remaining brown sugar. Broil 1-2 minutes longer or until bubbly. Cool for 2-3 minutes. Serve with ice cream; drizzle with butterscotch topping. **Yield:** 8 servings.

I found a recipe similar to this in a cookbook and made up my own variation. My husband always chuckles at me, because I seldom make a recipe as it is called for—I always think I have a better way!

**KAREN GRANT
TULARE, CALIFORNIA**

Pretty Slices of Angel Food Cake: **tip** With its airy texture, it can be difficult to slice angel food cake because it squashes under pressure. For perfect slices every time, use your electric knife.

chocolate brownie cookies

PREP: 20 MIN. + CHILLING BAKE: 10 MIN./BATCH

1/2	cup sugar
1	egg
2	tablespoons canola oil
1	square (1 ounce) unsweetened chocolate, melted and cooled
1/2	teaspoon vanilla extract
1/2	cup all-purpose flour
1/2	teaspoon baking powder
1/8	teaspoon salt

Confectioners' sugar

In a bowl, beat the sugar, egg, oil, chocolate and vanilla. Combine the flour, baking powder and salt; gradually add to creamed mixture. Chill for at least 2 hours.

Shape the dough into 1-in. balls; roll in confectioners' sugar. Place 2 in. apart on lightly greased baking sheets. Bake at 350° for 10-12 minutes or until set. Remove to wire racks. **Yield:** about 1 dozen.

These chocolaty cookies taste like brownies but are easier to hold and transport. Kids love the crackled confectioners' sugar coating.

RUTH CAIN
HARTSELLE, ALABAMA

DESERTS

sugar cookie tarts

PREP: 20 MIN. + CHILLING

5	tablespoons sugar, *divided*
1	teaspoon cornstarch

Dash salt

3	tablespoons water
2	tablespoons orange juice
1	tablespoon lemon juice
1	package (3 ounces) cream cheese, softened
4	large sugar cookies (3 inches)
1	cup sliced assorted fresh fruit (strawberries, kiwifruit *and/or* bananas)

For the glaze, in a small saucepan, combine 3 tablespoons sugar, cornstarch and salt. Gradually stir in the water, orange juice and lemon juice. Bring to a boil over medium heat; cook and stir for 2 minutes or until thickened. Remove from the heat; cool.

In a small bowl, beat cream cheese and remaining sugar until smooth. Spread over each cookie; arrange fruit on top. Drizzle with glaze. Refrigerate until chilled. **Yield:** 4 servings.

Purchased sugar cookies serve as the speedy "crust" for tasty tarts topped with cream cheese and fresh fruit.

BARB WHITE
LIGONIER, PENNSYLVANIA

mini rum cakes

PREP/TOTAL TIME: 10 MIN.

2	cups cold 2% milk
1	package (3.4 ounces) instant vanilla pudding mix
1	teaspoon rum extract
6	individual round sponge cakes
1-1/2	cups whipped topping

Fresh *or* frozen raspberries

In a small bowl, whisk the milk and pudding mix for 2 minutes; stir in rum extract. Let stand for 2 minutes or until soft-set.

Place sponge cakes on dessert plates; top with pudding. Garnish with whipped topping and raspberries. **Yield:** 6 servings.

My mother and I tried many different types of rum cake to find the best one, and finally hit on this cake. It doesn't dry out and imparts the most flavor. For a really moist cake, brush rum over the individual sponge cakes before topping them with the filling.

DONA HOFFMAN
ADDISON, ILLINOIS

Sweetened Whipped Cream:
Add a little extra sweetness to any dessert by garnishing with sweetened whipped cream. In a mixing bowl, whip 1 cup cream and 2 tablespoons confectioners' sugar on high until stiff peaks form.

lime parfaits

PREP/TOTAL TIME: 15 MIN.

1/2	cup plus 2 tablespoons chocolate wafer cookie crumbs, *divided*
1/4	cup finely chopped macadamia nuts, toasted
3	cups lime sherbet, softened
1	tablespoon grated lime peel

In a bowl, combine 1/2 cup cookie crumbs and nuts. In another bowl, combine sherbet and lime peel. Spoon 1 tablespoon cookie mixture into six parfait glasses; top with 1/4 cup sherbet mixture. Repeat layers. Sprinkle with remaining cookie crumbs. Cover and freeze until firm. **Yield:** 6 servings.

My refreshing, four-ingredient dessert is easy to prepare...and so pretty to serve. Layers of creamy ice-cold sherbet alternate with a crunchy combination of cookie crumbs and chopped nuts.

MITZI SENTIFF
ANNAPOLIS, MARYLAND

DESSERTS

chocolate orange pie

PREP: 20 MIN. + FREEZING

1	cup miniature marshmallows
1	cup (6 ounces) semisweet chocolate chips
1	cup evaporated milk
1	pint vanilla ice cream, softened
1	pint orange sherbet, softened
1	graham cracker crust (9 inches)
1/3	cup coarsely chopped pecans

In a saucepan, combine the marshmallows, chocolate chips and milk. Bring to a boil over medium heat; cook and stir for 2 minutes or until melted. Remove from the heat. Cool completely.

Meanwhile, alternately arrange scoops of ice cream and sherbet in the crust; smooth top. Pour the chocolate sauce over the pie; sprinkle with pecans. Cover and freeze for at least 4 hours. The pie may be frozen for up to 2 months. **Yield:** 6-8 servings.

I dreamed up this wonderful concoction when I was yearning for the creamy orange ice cream treat of my childhood. It's a make-ahead delight.

**LAURIE LACLAIR
NORTH RICHLAND HILLS
TEXAS**

apricot pumpkin cake

PREP: 5 MIN. BAKE: 25 MIN. + COOLING

1	cup chopped dried apricots
1	package (14 ounces) pumpkin quick bread/muffin mix
1	cup water
2	eggs
3	tablespoons canola oil
1	can (15 ounces) apricot halves, drained
1	can (16 ounces) cream cheese frosting
1/2	cup chopped pecans

Set aside 1/2 cup dried apricots for garnish. In a small bowl, soak remaining apricots in hot water for 5 minutes; drain well. Puree in a food processor or blender.

In a large bowl, combine the quick bread mix, water, eggs, oil and pureed apricots. Stir in the canned apricots. Pour into a greased 11-in. x 7-in. baking dish.

Bake at 375° for 22-27 minutes or until a toothpick inserted near the center comes out clean. Cool on a wire rack. Frost cake with cream cheese frosting; sprinkle with pecans and reserved apricots. Refrigerate leftovers. **Yield:** 9 servings.

Apricots combined with pumpkin quick bread mix makes a simply delicious, moist cake.

TASTE OF HOME
TEST KITCHEN

Homemade Cream Cheese Frosting: When time allows, make your own cream cheese frosting. In the microwave-safe bowl, soften two 3-ounce blocks of cream cheese and 3/4 cup butter; beat in 1 teaspoon vanilla extract. Gradually stir in 3 cups confectioners' sugar. Refrigerate until ready to use.

DESSERTS

creamy mango loaf cake

PREP: 20 MIN. + CHILLING

1-1/4	cups cold fat-free half-and-half
1	package (1 ounce) sugar-free instant vanilla pudding mix
1	medium mango, peeled and diced
1	loaf (10-1/2 ounces) angel food cake
1	medium kiwifruit, peeled and sliced

In a large bowl, whisk the half-and-half and pudding mix for 2 minutes. Let stand for 2 minutes or until soft-set. Fold in mango.

Cut the cake horizontally into three layers; spread the pudding mixture between layers and over top of cake. Top with the kiwi. Refrigerate for at least 4 hours before serving. **Yield:** 6 servings.

For a refreshing finale, I dress up prepared angel food cake with a handful of items; this recipe is the luscious result. If your family doesn't like mango, replace it with a cup of any other diced fruit. It tops off a meal deliciously.

**LINDA MCLYMAN
SYRACUSE, NEW YORK**

Use a Spoon to Peel Kiwi: First, cut off both ends of a kiwi that is ripe but not too soft. Slip a teaspoon just under the skin, matching the spoon's curve to the curve of the fruit. Slide the spoon around the kiwi to separate the fruit from the skin, being careful not to dig the spoon into the flesh. Once the spoon has been completely run around the fruit, it will easily slip out of the skin in one smooth piece.

banana snack cake

PREP: 10 MIN. BAKE: 30 MIN. + COOLING

1-2/3   cups all-purpose flour
1   teaspoon baking soda
1   cup packed brown sugar
1/2   cup water
1/3   cup mashed ripe bananas (about 1 small)
1/3   cup canola oil
1/2   teaspoon vanilla extract
Confectioners' sugar

In a bowl, combine flour and baking soda. In another bowl, whisk the brown sugar, water, banana, oil and vanilla. Stir into the dry ingredients just until moistened. Transfer to a greased 8-in. square baking dish.

Bake at 350° for 30-35 minutes or until a toothpick inserted near the center comes out clean. Cool on a wire rack. Dust with confectioners' sugar. Cut into squares. **Yield:** 9 servings.

EDITOR'S NOTE: This recipe does not use eggs.

This cake doesn't need any frosting—just a dusting of powdered sugar. Weekday guests are always amazed that I made this treat from scratch.

DENISE LOEWENTHAL
HINCKLEY, OHIO

DESERTS

granola banana sticks
PREP/TOTAL TIME: 20 MIN.

1/4	cup peanut butter
2	tablespoons plus 1-1/2 teaspoons honey
4-1/2	teaspoons brown sugar
2	teaspoons milk
3	medium firm bananas
6	Popsicle sticks
2	crunchy oat and honey granola bars, crushed

In a small saucepan, combine the peanut butter, honey, brown sugar and milk; cook until heated through, stirring occasionally.

Peel bananas and cut in half widthwise; insert a Popsicle stick into one end of each banana half. Spoon peanut butter mixture over bananas to coat completely. Sprinkle with granola. Serve immediately or place on a waxed paper-lined baking sheet and freeze. **Yield:** 6 servings.

My daughter and I won an award at our local fair for these peanut-butter-and-granola bananas. I like to assemble the ingredients ahead for my kids to whip up when they get home from school.
DIANE TOOMEY
ALLENTOWN, PENNSYLVANIA

Easy Substitution Idea:
As a crunchy alternative to the granola bars, make these banana treats with crisp rice cereal.

almond apricot bars

PREP: 15 MIN. BAKE: 45 MIN. + COOLING

2	cups vanilla chips *or* white chips, *divided*
1/2	cup butter, softened
1/2	cup sugar
2	eggs
1	teaspoon vanilla extract
1	cup all-purpose flour
3/4	cup apricot jam
1/2	cup sliced almonds

In a microwave, melt 1 cup chips; set aside. In a large bowl, cream butter and sugar until light and fluffy. Add eggs, one at a time, beating well after each addition. Beat in melted chips and vanilla. Gradually beat in flour. Spread half of the batter into a greased 8-in. square baking dish. Bake at 325° for 15-20 minutes or until golden brown. Spread with jam.

Stir remaining chips into remaining batter. Drop by tablespoonfuls over jam; carefully spread over top. Sprinkle with the almonds. Bake for 30-35 minutes or until golden brown. Cool completely on a wire rack. Cut into squares, then cut each diagonally. **Yield:** 1-1/2 dozen.

Apricot jam provides the fruit flavor in this small pan of sweet dessert bars. They're also good with seedless raspberry jam.

OLGA WOLKOSKY
RICHMOND
BRITISH COLUMBIA

DESSERTS

cream cheese cookie cups

PREP: 15 MIN. BAKE: 10 MIN. + COOLING

1	tube (18 ounces) refrigerated chocolate chip cookie dough
4	ounces cream cheese, softened
2	tablespoons butter, softened
1/2	teaspoon vanilla extract
1-1/4	cups confectioners' sugar

Cut cookie dough in half (save one portion for another use). With floured hands, press about 1 tablespoon of dough onto the bottom and up the sides of 12 ungreased miniature muffin cups. Bake at 350° for 8-10 minutes or until lightly browned.

Using the end of a wooden spoon handle, reshape the puffed cookie cups. Cool for 5 minutes before removing from pan to a wire rack to cool completely.

In a small bowl, beat the cream cheese, butter and vanilla until smooth. Gradually beat in confectioners' sugar. Spoon into cookie cups. Store in the refrigerator. **Yield:** 1 dozen.

Need a quick dessert? Try these yummy cookie bites. For a pretty look, use an icing bag to pipe the filling into the cups, then top each with mini M&M's.

**RACHEL BLACKSTON
MAUK, GEORGIA**

maple mousse

PREP: 30 MIN. + CHILLING

3/4	cup plus 6 teaspoons maple syrup, *divided*
3	egg yolks, lightly beaten
2	cups heavy whipping cream
2	tablespoons chopped hazelnuts, toasted

In a small saucepan over medium heat, heat 3/4 cup syrup just until it simmers. Reduce heat to low. Stir a small amount of hot syrup into egg yolks; return all to the pan, stirring constantly. Cook and stir until mixture is thickened and reaches 160°. Transfer to a large bowl; set bowl in ice water and stir for 2 minutes. Cool to room temperature.

In a large bowl, beat cream until stiff peaks form. Gently fold into the syrup mixture. Spoon into dessert dishes. Chill for at least 2 hours. Just before serving, drizzle with remaining syrup and sprinkle with hazelnuts. **Yield:** 6 servings.

I love to make this dessert with maple syrup produced in our area. It's a change from heavier cakes and pies—a refreshing ending to a holiday meal.

JANE FULLER
IVORYTON, CONNECTICUT

How to Handle Hazelnuts: You can easily remove skins from shelled hazelnuts and then enrich their flavor by toasting. Spread the nuts in a single layer in a baking pan. Bake at 350° for 10 to 15 minutes or until the nuts are toasted and the skins begin to flake. Transfer nuts to a clean kitchen towel; rub against the towel to remove skins.

DESSERTS

strawberry granola squares

PREP: 5 MIN. BAKE: 25 MIN. + COOLING

1-1/2	cups granola cereal without raisins
3/4	cup all-purpose flour
1/3	cup packed brown sugar
1/2	teaspoon ground cinnamon
5	tablespoons cold butter
1	cup strawberry preserves

In a large bowl, combine the granola, flour, brown sugar and cinnamon; cut in butter until crumbly. Set aside a third of the mixture for topping. Press remaining mixture into a well-greased 9-in. square baking pan. Bake at 375° for 10 minutes.

Spread preserves over crust; sprinkle with reserved granola mixture. Bake 15 minutes longer or until filling is bubbly around the edges. Cool on a wire rack. Cut into squares. Store in the refrigerator. **Yield:** 16 squares.

Most of the ingredients in these delicious squares can be found in your pantry. Make them ahead and freeze for a fast treat anytime.

**TASTE OF HOME
TEST KITCHEN**

Quickly Cut in Butter:
When making Strawberry Granola Squares or other recipes that call for cutting in cold butter, shred very cold butter on a flat cheese grater. This is much faster than cutting up the butter into workable pieces...and it blends perfectly into the dry ingredients.

pound cake with strawberries

PREP/TOTAL TIME: 5 MIN.

- 1   cup (8 ounces) sour cream
- 1   teaspoon sugar
- 1   loaf (10-3/4 ounces) frozen pound cake, thawed and cut into cubes
- 1   package (10 ounces) frozen sweetened sliced strawberries, thawed

In a small bowl, combine sour cream and sugar. Place cake cubes in dessert dishes; top with strawberries and sweetened sour cream. **Yield:** 8 servings.

You can put this sweet dessert together in a snap.

SUE ROSS
CASA GRANDE, ARIZONA

cocoa cake brownies

PREP/TOTAL TIME: 30 MIN.

- 1   cup butter, melted
- 1   cup sugar
- 4   eggs
- 2   teaspoons vanilla extract
- 1   cup all-purpose flour
- 7   tablespoons baking cocoa
- 1   teaspoon baking powder
- 1/2   teaspoon salt

In a bowl, combine the butter and sugar. Add eggs, one at a time, stirring well after each addition. Stir in vanilla. Combine the flour, cocoa, baking powder and salt. Gradually add to butter mixture; stir until moistened.

Transfer to a greased 13-in. x 9-in. baking pan. Bake at 350° for 20-25 minutes or until a toothpick inserted near the center comes out clean. Cool on a wire rack. **Yield:** about 2-1/2 dozen.

These brownies are delicious. They have a texture somewhere between chewy and cake-like brownies.

HELEN TURNER
UPLAND, INDIANA

cinnamon apple tartlets

PREP/TOTAL TIME: 15 MIN.

- 1   tube (8 ounces) refrigerated crescent rolls
- 4-1/2   teaspoons cinnamon-sugar, *divided*
- 1   large tart apple, thinly sliced

Separate crescent dough into four rectangles; place on an ungreased baking sheet. Seal the perforations. Sprinkle with 3 teaspoons cinnamon-sugar.

Bake at 375° for 5 minutes. Arrange apple slices over dough; sprinkle with remaining cinnamon-sugar. Bake 5-8 minutes longer or until golden brown. Serve warm. **Yield:** 4 servings.

The flaky treats are a fun ending to a great weeknight meal. And they come together in just about 15 minutes.

TASTE OF HOME
TEST KITCHEN

DESSERTS

lemon sorbet

PREP: 15 MIN. + FREEZING

1	cup sugar
1	cup water
3/4	cup lemon juice
3	tablespoons grated lemon peel

In a small saucepan over medium heat, cook and stir sugar and water until mixture comes to a boil. Reduce heat; simmer, uncovered, for 2 minutes. Remove from the heat; cool to room temperature.

Stir in the lemon juice and lemon peel. Freeze in an ice cream freezer according to manufacturer's directions. Transfer to a freezer container; freeze for at least 4 hours before serving. **Yield:** 2 cups.

This creamy, four-ingredient sorbet is both sweet and tart. It makes a delightfully refreshing finish to any meal.

**GOLDENE PETERSEN
BRIGHAM CITY, UTAH**

**Making
Lemon Boats:**
Cut a large lemon in half. If necessary, trim the bottom so it sits upright in a dish. Gently squeeze out the juice from each half. With a small scissors or knife, cut the membrane at each end to loosen the pulp from each shell. With your fingertips, pull membrane and pulp away from the shell. Place shells upside down on a damp paper towel and refrigerate until serving.

homemade ice cream sandwiches

PREP: 30 MIN. + FREEZING

2	tablespoons sugar
1-1/2	teaspoons cornstarch
1	tablespoon butter, melted
1/2	cup 2% milk
1/2	teaspoon vanilla extract
2/3	cup sweetened condensed milk
1	cup heavy whipping cream
1	ounce semisweet chocolate, melted
18	chocolate chip *or* sugar cookies (3 inches)

Miniature semisweet chocolate chips, chocolate jimmies, chopped unsalted peanuts *or* flaked coconut, optional

In a small saucepan, combine the sugar, cornstarch and butter; stir in milk. Bring to a boil over medium heat; cook and stir for 2 minutes or until thickened. Remove from the heat; stir in vanilla. Cool completely. Stir in condensed milk.

In a large bowl, beat cream until stiff peaks form; fold into milk mixture. Divide between two freezer containers. Stir melted chocolate into one container until well blended. Cover and freeze both mixtures for 6 hours or until firm.

To assemble, place 1/3 cup of ice cream on the bottom of a cookie. Top with another cookie; press down gently. If desired, roll sides of ice cream sandwich in chocolate chips, jimmies, peanuts or coconut. Wrap in plastic wrap. Repeat. Freeze until serving. **Yield:** 9 servings.

Served between your favorite bakery cookies, the easy ice cream in this recipe makes an irresistible dessert. The recipe comes together in a matter of minutes, then cools in your freezer for yummy enjoyment anytime.

TASTE OF HOME
TEST KITCHEN

fruity cereal bars

PREP/TOTAL TIME: 30 MIN.

3	tablespoons butter
1	package (10 ounces) large marshmallows
6	cups crisp rice cereal
1/2	cup dried chopped apple
1/2	cup dried cranberries

In a large saucepan, combine butter and marshmallows. Cook and stir over medium-low heat until melted. Remove from the heat; stir in the cereal, apples and cranberries.

Pat into a 13-in. x 9-in. pan coated with cooking spray; cool. Cut into squares. **Yield:** 20 servings.

With dried apple and cranberries, these crispy cereal bars are perfect for snacks or brown-bag lunches. Store the extras in plastic containers—that is, if you have any left!

GIOVANNA KRANENBERG
CAMBRIDGE, MINNESOTA

DESSERTS

doughnut parfaits

PREP/TOTAL TIME: 20 MIN.

2 cups cold milk
1 package (3.4 ounces) instant vanilla pudding mix
16 powdered sugar doughnut holes, halved
1 to 2 medium firm bananas, cut into 1/4-inch slices
2 cups whipped topping
Chopped nuts and maraschino cherries

In a large bowl, whisk the milk and pudding mix for 2 minutes. Let stand for 2 minutes or until soft-set. Place four doughnut hole halves in each of four parfait glasses. Top with half of the pudding, bananas and whipped topping. Repeat layers. Garnish with nuts and cherries. **Yield:** 4 servings.

I was in a hurry to make a quick dessert, so I threw together a few items from the grocery store. My whole family raved about the results.

CHRISTINE DELILI
VON LAKE, OHIO

Skip the Parfaits: Instead of making individual parfaits, layer the pudding, bananas and whipped topping in a clear glass bowl for an impressive yet timeless trifle. It's so easy you can even enlist the kids to assemble it!

chocolate silk pie

PREP: 30 MIN. + CHILLING

1   unbaked pastry shell (9 inches)
1   jar (7 ounces) marshmallow creme
1   cup (6 ounces) semisweet chocolate chips
1/4   cup butter, cubed
2   ounces unsweetened chocolate
2   tablespoons strong brewed coffee
1   cup heavy whipping cream, whipped

TOPPING:
1   cup heavy whipping cream
2   tablespoons confectioners' sugar
Chocolate curls, optional

Line unpricked pastry shell with a double thickness of heavy-duty foil. Bake at 450° for 8 minutes. Remove foil; bake 5 minutes longer. Cool on a wire rack.

Meanwhile, in a heavy saucepan, combine the marshmallow creme, chocolate chips, butter, unsweetened chocolate and coffee; cook and stir over low heat until chocolate is melted and mixture is smooth. Cool. Fold in whipped cream; pour into crust.

For topping, in a large bowl, beat cream until it begins to thicken. Add confectioners' sugar; beat until stiff peaks form. Spread over filling. Refrigerate for at least 3 hours before serving. Garnish with chocolate curls if desired. **Yield:** 6-8 servings.

This creamy chocolate pie not only melts in your mouth, it also melts any and all resistance to dessert!

MARY RELYEA
CANASTOTA, NEW YORK

DESSERTS

no-bake apple pie

PREP: 20 MIN. + CHILLING

5	medium tart apples, peeled and sliced
1-3/4	cups water, *divided*
1	package (.3 ounce) sugar-free lemon gelatin
1/2	teaspoon ground cinnamon
1/4	teaspoon ground nutmeg
1	package (0.8 ounce) sugar-free cook-and-serve vanilla pudding mix
1/2	cup chopped nuts
1	reduced-fat graham cracker crust (8 inches)
1/2	cup fat-free whipped topping

In a large saucepan, combine the apples, 1-1/2 cups water, gelatin, cinnamon and nutmeg. Bring to a boil. Reduce heat; cover and simmer for 4-6 minutes or until apples are tender.

Combine dry pudding mix and remaining water; add to the apple mixture. Cook for 1 minute or until thickened. Remove from the heat; stir in nuts. Pour into the crust. Refrigerate for at least 2 hours before serving. Garnish with whipped topping. **Yield:** 8 servings.

We always have an abundance of apples in the fall, so I like to make this easy pie. My husband is diabetic, and this recipe fits into his diet...but everyone enjoys it.

SHIRLEY VREDENBURG
OSSINEKE, MICHIGAN

surprise cookie pops

PREP/TOTAL TIME: 25 MIN. 30〉

2	Milky Way candy bars (2.05 ounces *each*)
12	Popsicle sticks
1	tube (18 ounces) chocolate chip cookie dough

Cut each candy bar widthwise into six pieces; insert a Popsicle stick into each. Cut cookie dough into 12 pieces. Flatten dough; wrap each piece around each candy bar piece, forming a ball.

Place 3 in. apart on ungreased baking sheets. Bake at 350° for 13-15 minutes or until lightly browned. Cool for 3 minutes before removing to wire racks. **Yield:** 1 dozen.

You will only need two ingredients—and some Popsicle sticks—to make this fun dessert. Store-bought dough and candy bars combine for a dozen sweet treats that will have your kids reaching for more.

**TASTE OF HOME
TEST KITCHEN**

Bake Sale Favorite: Do you have a bake sale coming up? Double the recipe for Surprise Cookie Pops. Wrap the baked cookies individually in cellophane bags. Tie ribbon around the sticks to secure.

DESERTS

fun fruit dessert

PREP/TOTAL TIME: 20 MIN.

1	cup vanilla yogurt
1	tablespoon honey
1	to 2 tablespoons minced fresh mint
3/4	cup chopped peeled peaches *or* nectarines
1-1/2	teaspoons orange juice
3/4	cup chopped fresh strawberries
3/4	cup fresh raspberries
3/4	cup fresh blueberries
1	tablespoon sugar
1	package (3.78 ounces) curved chocolate slices (Swoops)

In a small bowl, combine the yogurt, honey and mint. Cover and refrigerate until serving.

Just before serving, place peaches in a large bowl; sprinkle with orange juice. Add the berries. Sprinkle with sugar; toss gently. Using a slotted spoon, transfer fruit to a serving bowl. Serve with yogurt sauce and chocolate slices. **Yield:** 6 servings.

This colorful, fruit-filled dish is perfect for any summer gathering. Served with a touch of chocolate, it makes an elegant treat with kid-friendly appeal.

**TASTE OF HOME
TEST KITCHEN**

creamy cappuccino mousse

PREP: 20 MIN. + CHILLING

1	package (8 ounces) cream cheese, softened
1/2	cup cold milk
1	cup strong brewed coffee, room temperature
1	package (3.4 ounces) instant vanilla pudding mix
1/4	teaspoon ground cinnamon
1	carton (8 ounces) frozen whipped topping, thawed, *divided*

Additional ground cinnamon

In a large bowl, beat the cream cheese until smooth. Gradually beat in milk until blended. Gradually beat in coffee. Add pudding mix and cinnamon; whisk for 2 minutes. Let stand for 5 minutes or until soft-set.

Fold in 2 cups whipped topping. Spoon into six dessert dishes. Refrigerate until set. Garnish with remaining whipped topping and additional cinnamon. **Yield:** 6 servings.

This smooth coffee mousse is simple to prepare and very delicious. I also think it would be good layered with pound cake in a trifle bowl.

BRENDA JACKSON
GARDEN CITY, KANSAS

Save Some of Your Morning Coffee:
After brewing a pot of coffee in the morning, set aside 1 cup for Creamy Cappuccino Mousse. Cover and refrigerate until ready to use. Reheat slightly to bring to room temperature.

chocolate swirl delight

PREP: 20 MIN. + CHILLING

1	package (13 ounces) Swiss cake rolls
2-3/4	cups cold milk
2	packages (3.9 ounces *each*) instant chocolate fudge pudding mix
2	cups whipped topping

Cut each cake roll into eight slices; set aside any chocolate coating that separates from rolls for garnish. Line a 9-in. springform pan with cake slices, completely covering the bottom and sides.

In a small bowl, whisk milk and pudding mixes for 2 minutes. Let stand for 2 minutes or until soft-set. Pour over cake. Spread with whipped topping; sprinkle with any of the reserved chocolate coating.

Cover and refrigerate for at least 2 hours before serving. **Yield:** 12 servings.

I made a few alterations to a great recipe and ended up with an impressive dessert. Everyone loves its light texture and chocolaty flavor.

LYNNE BARGAR
SAEGERTOWN, PENNSYLVANIA

DESSERTS

watermelon granita

PREP: 15 MIN. + FREEZING

1-1/4	cups sugar
1-1/4	cups water
6	cups cubed watermelon

Small watermelon wedges, optional

In a small saucepan, bring sugar and water to a boil. Cook and stir until the sugar is dissolved; set aside. In a blender, process watermelon in batches until smooth. Strain; discard pulp and seeds. Transfer to an 8-in. square dish; stir in sugar mixture. Cool to room temperature.

Freeze for 1 hour; stir with a fork. Freeze 2-3 hours longer or until completely frozen, stirring every 30 minutes. Stir granita with a fork just before serving; spoon into dessert dishes. Garnish with melon wedges if desired. **Yield:** 8 servings.

Say a sweet "ciao" to summer with this light and airy Italian treat! Serve in pretty glasses garnished with wedges of cantaloupe or mint sprigs.

**TASTE OF HOME
TEST KITCHEN**

**Learn More
About Melon:** Although watermelons are available year-round, they're at their peak May through September. Select melons with a hard, green rind that has a dull appearance. The color of the part that rested on the ground will be creamy yellow or white. To test for ripeness, slap the side of the melon with your palm. A deep thump means it's ripe. You should get about 1 cup cubed fruit from every pound.

old-fashioned rhubarb pudding cake

PREP: 30 MIN. BAKE: 30 MIN. + COOLING

4	cups diced fresh *or* frozen rhubarb
1-1/2	cups sugar, *divided*
1/4	cup shortening
1	egg
1/2	teaspoon vanilla extract
1	cup all-purpose flour
2	teaspoons baking powder
1/4	teaspoon salt
1/2	cup milk

In a large saucepan, combine the rhubarb and 1 cup sugar. Cook over medium heat for 12-15 minutes or until rhubarb is tender.

Meanwhile, in a small bowl, cream shortening and remaining sugar until light and fluffy; beat in egg and vanilla. Combine the flour, baking powder and salt; add to creamed mixture alternately with milk. Beat just until combined.

Pour into a greased 9-in. square baking dish. Pour rhubarb mixture over batter. Bake at 350° for 30-35 minutes or until a toothpick inserted near the center comes out clean. Cool on a wire rack. **Yield:** 9 servings.

I have fond memories enjoying this comforting dessert while growing up. It's one of my mom's best recipes.

BARBARA COLLINS
ANDOVER, MASSACHUSETTS

DESSERTS

 ## mocha pudding cakes

PREP/TOTAL TIME: 30 MIN.

1/4	cup all-purpose flour
3	tablespoons sugar
1-1/2	teaspoons baking cocoa
1/2	teaspoon baking powder
1/8	teaspoon salt
3	tablespoons 2% milk
1-1/2	teaspoons butter, melted
1/4	teaspoon vanilla extract

TOPPING:

2	tablespoons brown sugar
1-1/2	teaspoons baking cocoa
3	tablespoons hot brewed coffee
1	tablespoon hot water

Whipped topping, optional

In a small bowl, combine the flour, sugar, cocoa, baking powder and salt. Stir in the milk, butter and vanilla until smooth. Spoon into two 4-oz. ramekins or custard cups coated with cooking spray.

Combine brown sugar and cocoa; sprinkle over batter. Combine coffee and water; pour over topping. Bake at 350° for 15-20 minutes or until a knife inserted near the center comes out clean. Serve warm or at room temperature with whipped topping if desired. **Yield:** 2 servings.

Mouthwatering mini cakes are the perfect treat for a twosome. My mom used to make these when I was a little girl. Now I whip them up for a speedy dessert.

DEBORA SIMMONS
EGLON, WEST VIRGINIA

banana cream dessert

PREP: 15 MIN. + CHILLING

4	medium firm bananas, sliced
1/2	cup lemon juice
1-1/2	cups graham cracker crumbs (about 24 squares)
1/4	cup sugar
1/2	cup butter, melted
1	cup (8 ounces) sour cream
1	package (3.4 ounces) instant vanilla pudding mix
1	carton (12 ounces) frozen whipped topping, thawed
1/3	cup chopped pecans

Toss bananas with lemon juice; drain well and set aside. In a bowl, combine the cracker crumbs, sugar and butter. Press into a greased 9-in. springform pan.

In a small bowl, beat the sour cream and pudding mix on low speed for 2 minutes. Fold in bananas and whipped topping. Pour into prepared crust. Chill for up to 6 hours. Sprinkle with pecans. **Yield:** 8-10 servings.

I rely on bananas, instant pudding mix and whipped topping to make this refreshing treat.

ANGEL HALL
GRAYVILLE, ILLINOIS

Keep Cracker Crumbs on Hand: Purchased graham cracker crumbs make for even easier assembly of Banana Cream Dessert. Look for them in your grocery store's baking aisle. They can be used in a variety of desserts.

DESSERTS

berry refresher dessert

PREP/TOTAL TIME: 10 MIN.

1	quart pineapple *or* lemon sherbet
1	cup sliced fresh strawberries
1/2	cup blueberries
1/2	cup white grape juice *or* white wine

Divide the sherbet among six dessert cups or bowls. Top with the berries and grape juice. **Yield:** 6 servings.

This colorful combination of pineapple sherbet, berries and grape juice makes a refreshing dessert on a hot summer day.

CAROL GILLESPIE
CHAMBERSBURG
PENNSYLVANIA

Buying and Storing Strawberries:
Purchase the plumpest and most fragrant berries. They should be firm, bright and fresh-looking, with no mold or bruised spots. The berries may have a little green or white color at the very top. Refrigerate unwashed berries in a paper towel-lined, moisture-proof container for 2 to 3 days. Wash when ready to use.

caramel toffee bombe

PREP: 15 MIN. + FREEZING

3/4	cup crushed gingersnaps (about 14 cookies)
3	tablespoons butter, melted
1	pint vanilla ice cream, softened
2	Heath candy bars (1.4 ounces *each*), chopped
1/3	cup caramel ice cream topping, warmed

Line a 3-cup bowl with plastic wrap. Combine cookie crumbs and butter; press onto the bottom and up the sides of prepared bowl. In a large bowl, beat ice cream and chopped candy bars until blended; spoon into crust. Cover and freeze until firm.

Trim edge of crust even with ice cream if necessary. Invert onto a serving platter; remove plastic wrap. Let stand 10 minutes before cutting. Drizzle with the caramel topping. **Yield:** 4-6 servings.

I need only five ingredients to put together this impressive dessert. Gingersnap cookies form the full-flavored "shell" over vanilla ice cream dressed up with crushed toffee candy bars.

CHERYL MILLER
FORT COLLINS, COLORADO

chocolate peanut butter mousse

PREP: 15 MIN. + CHILLING

1	milk chocolate candy bar (5 ounces), chopped
1	cup heavy whipping cream
1	cup creamy peanut butter
1/3	cup chocolate-covered peanuts, chopped

In a microwave-safe bowl, combine the candy bar, cream and peanut butter. Microwave at 50% power for 2-3 minutes or until smooth, stirring twice. Transfer to a small bowl. Cover and refrigerate for 1 hour or until chilled.

Beat until soft peaks form. Spoon into dessert dishes; sprinkle with the chocolate-covered peanuts. **Yield:** 6 servings.

EDITOR'S NOTE: This recipe was tested in a 1,100-watt microwave.

This dessert combines chocolate and peanut butter perfectly. It's ideal for summer night entertaining and · a nice alternative to ice cream.

MARIA REGAKIS
SOMERVILLE, MASSACHUSETTS

DESERTS

cheesecake waffle cups

PREP/TOTAL TIME: 10 MIN.

1	package (8 ounces) cream cheese, softened
1	can (14 ounces) sweetened condensed milk
1/3	cup lemon juice
1	teaspoon vanilla extract
4	waffle bowls
1	cup cherry pie filling

In a small bowl, beat the cream cheese until smooth. Gradually beat in the milk until smooth. Stir in the lemon juice and vanilla. Spoon about 1/3 cup into each waffle bowl; top with 2 tablespoons of pie filling. Repeat layers. **Yield:** 4 servings.

I've found a fun way to serve cheesecake. The crunchy store-bought bowls hold a smooth cream cheese filling that's layered with cherry pie filling. They're a snap to prepare and are attractive, too. Blueberry pie filling would be a nice alternative.

JANICE GREENHALGH
FLORENCE, KENTUCKY

almond cookies

PREP: 10 MIN.
BAKE: 10 MIN./BATCH + COOLING

1	cup shortening
1/2	cup plus 3 tablespoons sugar, *divided*
1/4	cup packed brown sugar
1	egg
1	teaspoon almond extract
2	cups all-purpose flour
1-1/2	teaspoons baking powder
1/8	teaspoon salt
3	tablespoons sliced almonds

In a small bowl, cream the shortening, 1/2 cup sugar and brown sugar. Beat in egg and extract.

Combine the flour, baking powder and salt; gradually add to the creamed mixture; mix well. Shape into 1-in. balls. Roll in remaining sugar.

Place 2 in. apart on ungreased baking sheets. Flatten with the bottom of a glass. Press three almond slices into the center of each.

Bake at 350° for 9-11 minutes or until edges are lightly browned. Cool for 2 minutes before removing to wire racks. **Yield:** 3 dozen.

I started making these cookies after enjoying similar ones at my favorite Chinese restaurant. They're crisp and have a wonderful almond flavor.

BEVERLY PRESTON
FOND DU LAC, WISCONSIN

Shortening Secrets: Butter or stick margarine can be substituted for shortening in equal proportions in cookie recipes. Most folks prefer butter because of the wonderful flavor it imparts. However, you can expect some changes in the texture of your baked goods. Cookies made with butter will have a darker color and tend to spread out more as they bake. Using part butter and part shortening will help cookies keep their shape.

simple snowflakes

PREP/TOTAL TIME: 25 MIN.

6	flour tortillas (6 inches), warmed
2	teaspoons canola oil

Confectioners' sugar

Fold a tortilla in half, then in half again and once again. Using a clean scissors or sharp knife, cut small triangles on folded and outside edges. Unfold tortilla; brush both sides with oil. Place on a greased baking sheet. Repeat with the remaining tortillas and oil.

Bake at 400° for 7-8 minutes or until lightly browned. Dust both sides of the tortillas with confectioners' sugar while they're still warm. **Yield:** 6 servings.

To make these treats, I simply cut tortillas into flake shapes, bake and dust them with sugar. Enlist the kids to help while you focus on dinner!

DENIS ANN BONTRAGER
GOSHEN, INDIANA

DESSERTS

sour cream cranberry bars

PREP: 15 MIN. BAKE: 30 MIN. + COOLING

1	cup butter, softened
1	cup packed brown sugar
2	cups quick-cooking oats
1-1/2	cups plus 2 tablespoons all-purpose flour, *divided*
2	cups dried cranberries
1	cup (8 ounces) sour cream
3/4	cup sugar
1	egg, lightly beaten
1	tablespoon grated lemon peel
1	teaspoon vanilla extract

In a large bowl, cream butter and brown sugar until light and fluffy. Combine oats and 1-1/2 cups flour; add to the creamed mixture until blended. Set aside 1-1/2 cups for the topping.

Press remaining crumb mixture into an ungreased 13-in. x 9-in. baking pan. Bake at 350° for 10-12 minutes or until lightly browned.

Meanwhile, in a large bowl, combine the cranberries, sour cream, sugar, egg, lemon peel, vanilla and remaining flour. Spread evenly over crust. Sprinkle with reserved crumb mixture.

Bake for 20-25 minutes or until lightly browned. Cool on a wire rack. Refrigerate leftovers. **Yield:** about 3 dozen.

A filling made with dried cranberries is layered between a buttery crust and a golden crumb topping in these flavorful bars.

**BARBARA NOWAKOWSKI
MESA, ARIZONA**

Measuring Brown Sugar: Brown sugar should always be firmly packed when being measured. The moisture in brown sugar tends to trap air between the crystals.

creamy banana-berry pie

PREP: 30 MIN. + CHILLING

1	sheet refrigerated pie pastry
1/4	cup chopped pecans
1-1/4	cups cold fat-free milk
1/2	cup reduced-fat sour cream

Sugar substitute equivalent to 1/4 cup sugar

1	package (.9 ounce) sugar-free instant banana pudding mix
2	cups reduced-fat whipped topping
1	tablespoon lemon juice
2	medium bananas
1/3	cup fresh blueberries

Unroll pastry on a lightly floured surface. Sprinkle with pecans; lightly roll pecans into pastry. Transfer to a 9-in. pie plate. Line unpricked pastry shell with a double thickness of heavy-duty foil. Bake at 450° for 8 minutes. Remove foil; bake 5 minutes longer. Cool on a wire rack.

In a small bowl, combine the milk, sour cream and sugar substitute. Gradually whisk in pudding mix. Fold in whipped topping.

Place lemon juice in a small bowl. Slice bananas into juice and stir gently to coat. Set aside 1/3 cup; spoon remaining banana slices into the crust. Top with pudding mixture, blueberries and reserved banana slices. Cover and refrigerate for 30 minutes before serving. **Yield:** 8 servings.

EDITOR'S NOTE: This recipe was tested with Splenda no-calorie sweetener.

Cool, creamy and topped with bananas and fresh blueberries, this pretty pie is lighter than air and sure to please everyone's palate.

TASTE OF HOME
TEST KITCHEN

GENERAL INDEX

cinnamon apple tartlets, pg. 219

mocha pudding cakes, pg. 230

GENERAL INDEX

grape tomato mozzarella salad, pg. 148

GENERAL INDEX

crepes with berries, pg. 94

GENERAL INDEX

ICE CREAM & SORBET

LEMON & LIME

MUFFINS

MUSHROOMS

NUTS & PEANUT BUTTER

ORANGES & NECTARINES

artichoke turkey salami salad, pg. 149

PASTA & NOODLES

GENERAL INDEX

turkey meatball soup, pg. 134

GENERAL INDEX

hot turkey bunwiches, pg. 118

ALPHABETICAL INDEX

baby carrots with almonds, pg. 172

ALPHABETICAL INDEX

dark chocolate fondue, pg. 198

D

F

ALPHABETICAL INDEX

frosty key lime pie, pg. 197

ALPHABETICAL INDEX

rhubarb cream muffins, pg. 110

ALPHABETICAL INDEX

salisbury steak with gemelli, pg. 54

RECIPE TIME INDEX

cinnamon peach enchiladas, pg. 204

RECIPE TIME INDEX

30 MINUTE RECIPES

RECIPE TIME INDEX

ginger beef stir-fry, pg. 44

RECIPE TIME INDEX

reuben chowder, pg. 146